# THE DARK EDGE

-

## OF AFRICAN LITERATURE

Smith and Ce {ed.]

AFRICAN
Library of Critical Writing

THE DARK EDGE - of African Literature
Smith and Ce (Ed.)

©African Library of Critical Writing
Print Edition
ISBN: 978-9-7837-0855-6

For information address:
Progeny (Press) International
Email: progeny.int@gmail.com
For: African Books Network
9 Handel Str.
AI EBS Nigeria WA
Email: handelbook@gmail.com


Marketing and Distribution in the US, UK,
Europe, N. America (Canada),
and Commonwealth countries by
 African Books Collective Ltd.
PO Box 721
Oxford OX1 9EN
United Kingdom
Email: orders@africanbookscollective.com

# Contents

# Introduction

CONTEMPORARY literatures of Africa add specificity on issues of conflicts, discords and the resultant tensions wrought upon individual and family on national and continental scales. *THE DARK EDGE of African Literature* proposes arguments and theories for the interpretation or exposition of Africa's modern fictions irrespective of the language of narrative. It attempts to discern how such interpretations of contemporary history may be received from an African perspective or what implications for African cultures and literatures abound by such experience. It is gladdening when these enquiries yield wider latitude of perspectives on African literature from as far as the United Kingdom, Africa, Asia, and America emerging in Nation/ Politics and the Writer's Forum.

"The Writer's Forum" presents the subject of "Two Africas and the Writer." It talks about the "Africa of the predators and the Africa of the prey," noting that the "mutual embedding of the realities of the concrete physical world of Africa and the continent's literature into each other also explains the striking similarities in the works of most modern African writers."

The Second Part studies the violence and conflicts of African Nations /Politics in literature. It contextualises that "texts can be interpreted only when they are placed against the backgrounds from which they emanate" and investigates "the controversy about the relational quality and dependent nature of text on context, and the exigency that informs the deliberate distortions of certain figures and images by contemporary African playwrights." The physical and psychological dislocation by war and violence of our individual and continental existence inspires studious research on *Maps*. The chapter "Defining the Other" takes the reader on a journey into the labyrinth of a young man's mind "back and forth from the time of his birth to the time of his adulthood in an attempt to find his identity."

This is analogous to tracing how African writing relates the subject matter of their works "to significant events that have taken place in their societies." The treatment of the Mau Mau uprising in Kenya, for instance, "reveals the links between cultural production and its ideological determinants in African literature." Yet "while attention has most often been focused on Ngugi wa Thiong'o", critics have often shied from examining the "veritable historical episode in the fiction of Meja Mwangi" whose status "excels in presenting many different, if often unrecognised, materials on the (Mau-Mau) uprising to readers of African literature."

"Voices: Crying in the Desert" is the chapter that deals with the history of Angolan literature through three epochs of "Brazilian Romanticism," "Portuguese Realism," and "Full Nativism." As argued, the third and current phase, which, by the way, echoes much of Negritude and Afrocentrism, is "marked by the claim to equality, fraternity and "a conscious and peremptory attitude inclined toward autonomist pretensions." This third and current stage "inherited the legacy of their predecessors and developed different forms of civic struggle." The chapter is quite a helpful introduction to the literary history of the Lusophone country of Angola.

The sixth chapter "Violence as Metaphor" links this search for identity in the midst of chaos and violence with "images of postcolonial violence that has modern African states such as Nigeria in a vice grip perennially threatening to consume the national cultural and political ethos of the entire African region." In this study of *Gamji College* the chapter fulfils the objectives of identifying, "the story-teller's conceptualisation of violence, and how it envelopes his narrative, characterization and language in a way that brings out the message in its glaring entirety."

An ending note to this section is "Representing Conflict," which examines the category of conflict in *Dance Under the Rain*, its conceptualisation of the inner schisms in post-independent Sudanese society, "particularly the seemingly unending North-South interface, the violent racial conflict between the black- and Arab-Sudanese, the inscription and circumscription of gender by nationalism and the overall shifting identities of postcolonial Sudanese modernities."

*- CS and CC*

# Writers' Forum

# Chapter 1

## *Two Africas and the Writer*

J. Ushie

PRE-colonial Africa had pre-capitalist class structures ranging from slave ownership to feudalism. But following colonialism and the subsequent ersatz independence, much of the continent bifurcated into two distinct worlds – the neo-colonialist and the post-colonialist – within the same geographical space. Neo-colonialist Africa is led by the surrogates of former colonial masters and other foreign interests while the continent's intellectual class leads on the post-colonialist front. Between these two "Africas" have been socio-economic and political crises that have resulted in the stagnation of the continent's growth and development. Using the dual perspectives of post-colonial and neo-colonial studies, this paper portrays the traumatizing impact of the neo-colonialist leadership on Africa's creative writers as a strand of the continent's intellectual class striving for genuine independence. It shows the African writer as a frequent site for the clashes in the struggle by post-colonialist Africans to wrest true independence from the grip of neo-colonialist leadership. It further traces this rift to the realities of Western capitalism's predatory domination of Africa, which began with the brutalizing commodification of Africans as slaves, was followed by the arbitrary creation of unworkable states, and now has reincarnated in neo-colonialism's garb and submits that the true and lasting peace and harmony can be achieved by the human race only if western capitalism and advances in science and technology are aligned with the pre-industrial, pre-capitalist and pre-racialist human values.

Two Africas in One

In Africa, whether in orate pre-colonial period or after, literature has never been a phenomenon detachable from the material realities of the society in which it is produced. The umbilical cord between the material world and the fictional world of literature is never severed, as the literature continues to feed on this physical world, which it, at the same time, interrogates, ridicules, satirizes or praises when praise is deserved. A literary work in Africa and the realities of its concrete world are, hence, necessarily mutually embedded in each other.

In most pre-colonial African worlds, there were folktales, legends, myths, proverbs and various forms of the song as an important literary sub-genre. In the traditional world of the people of the present Obudu and Obanliku areas of Nigeria, for example, the song was a major medium of social engineering and criticism. In this tradition, not even burial songs were always carriers of just the usual emotion-laden words of sympathy or sorrow. The tongue of the singer at the burial of a thief or of one who had died in any other species of dishonourable circumstances never failed to inflict deep wounds of shame in the deceased and, sometimes, in his/her entire family or community as a whole. E. O. Apronti notes that in serenading the king of the Ashanti, in Ghana, to his palace, the singer reminded him that he was the servant of the ruled "by singing the type of text to which he must stand at attention" and be delayed to test his "obedience" (qtd in Ushie 22).

It was this role of the artist in his society as social critic and 'righter' that explains the belligerence of the early modern African writer in his anti-colonial battle. In East Africa, for instance, land as the central issue was given its due prominence in Ngugi wa Thiong'o's *Weep Not, child* while Chinua Achebe, Wole Soyinka and other Anglophone West African writers consciously glorified their African indigenous culture in the bid to help their African readers to regain pride and confidence in their cultural heritage. In Francophone African countries, where the French policy of assimilation had more consciously sought to obliterate the African culture, the African anti-colonialist writers responded with the equally more corrosive concept of Negritude as we find in Camara Laye's *The African Child*, Mongo Beti's *Mission to Kala*, Ferdinand Oyono's *Houseboy* and in the poetry of Leopold Senghor. In South Africa, the poet, Dennis Brutus, and novelists like Peter Abrahams and Alex La Guma tore the robes off the apartheid policy with their literary works.

Following this role of the African writer, which effectively complemented the political flank in the struggle for independence, ersatz freedom came for the various African States. Most of them became independent in the 1960s while Lusophone Angola, Mozambique and Guinea-Bissau freed themselves from Portuguese control only in the 1970s. The apartheid regime of South Africa also grudgingly came to an end in 1994, when the first free-for-all elections were held. This then shows modern African literature's continuity from, and faithfulness to, its oral antecedents in the pre-colonial era.

Africa and Neo-Colonialism

In spite of the collective struggle for independence by Africans, and the euphoria that followed its attainment, what the vast majority of the people did not know was that it was a mere treacherous exchange of batons between out-going master and his few trusted heirs. Among the Bendi community in Nigeria it was told that when the first colonialists sought for men with whom to work they resolved not to send any of their worthy sons to them. Instead, only men whose identity in the community was doubtful, or who were loafers or scoundrels, were made over to the strangers. The thinking was that whatever the whites would do to those men could not affect the community very much. On the contrary, these men, whose exit from the community was a symbolic emptying of the community's garbage bin into the white man's travel bag, returned to the community as overlords. They returned as tax agents and court messengers, and, armoured by the new laws and authority, they treated the community without the usual African fellow feeling: their powers and positions had come from elsewhere outside the clan, not from within it. This, perhaps, explains why even today the loyalty of their neo-colonialist heirs remains to this external authority in Europe and America and not to the African community. It was these men or their children, who had come to constitute the first harvest of Africans into western ways – ways that dominated the African political and economic leadership class of the colonial days. Examples of fictional representations of these men in anti-colonial African literature are Lakunle in Wole Soyinka's play, *The Lion and the Jewel*, whose ways are plastic and his language flowery but without effect, compared to warm, old Baroka, the typical African whose actions are result-oriented. In Ngugi Wa Thiong'o's *Weep Not, child* there is Jacobo, who treats other Kenyans with disdain and takes sides with the white settlers against the rest of Kenyans during the Mau-Mau struggle for independence. Obi Okonkwo, who becomes baptized as Isaac in Chinua Achebe's novel, *No Longer at Ease*, is another example. And in apartheid South Africa, the black African policeman is, of course, on the side of the whites, under whose command and power he brutalizes his fellow Africans in various South African novels. These early converts into western ways thus became the colonialists' arsenal in the war against African culture and religion, which they worked assiduously to replace with Christianity and foreign culture.

In some cases the gulf between this early elite class and the rest of the Africans was blurred during the struggle for independence and immediately after. This, for instance, explains why post-independence rulers, such as Kenya's Jomo Kenyatta in Ngugi's *Weep Not, child*, were the people's heroes. Sartre summarizes the situation most aptly:

> The European elite undertook to manufacture a native elite. They picked out promising adolescents; they branded them, as with a red-hot iron, with the principles of western culture; they stuffed their mouths full with high-sounding phrases, grand glutinous words that stuck to the teeth. After a short stay in the mother's country they were sent home,

white-washed. These walking lies had nothing left to
say to their brothers; they only echoed. (Fanon 7)

Indeed, soon after Gabon's flag independence, a former
president of the country, Monsieur M'ba, assured his former
French masters, "Gabon is independent, but between Gabon
and France nothing has changed; everything goes on as
before" (Fanon 52). Symbolically, the experiences of
Kenya's writer, Gakaara wa Wanjau, also tie Africa's
colonial period to the neo-colonial: he was imprisoned in
both eras, thus showing the continuity of both colonialism
and the African writer's resistance to it even in the period
following flag independence. Nothing has changed indeed
in most African countries after foreign domination except
the skin colour of the exploiter. The African leaders who
took over the reins of power have thus been nothing but
mere reincarnations of the African middlemen of the slave
trade era, and crude surrogates of the former colonizers,
whose primary goal in politics has been the prebendal
lucre.

This failure of Africa's former colonies to sever their
umbilical cords with the erstwhile mother countries and
reposition themselves towards autarky is what defines a
neo-colonial state. A post-colonial state, on the contrary,
may have scars to show from erstwhile domination, but
would have a visible path towards self-reliance as an
independent state. Neo-colonial states such as we have in
Africa, have only reeking and profusely bleeding wounds to
show for their freedom, not yet scars. Africa was therefore
directly bled to the marrow by the colonial masters in the
heydays of colonialism, and lavishly infested with
visionless and maniacal thieves for political leaders in the
neo-colonial days. Taking both the first-tier of civilian

dictators and their subsequent military counterparts together, as in some cases, we have the representative examples of Francisco Macias Nguema, who ruled Equatorial Guinea for eleven years, and thereafter declared himself "Life President", "Leader of Steel" and the "Unique Miracle of Africa". There was Central African Republic's Jean-Bedel Bokassa, who was said to have fed dissidents to lions and, in 1979, killed some 100 school children for protesting against a certain school uniform. Indeed, on one occasion, he was reported to have stated:

> I am the head and ruler of a nation of thieves. To keep them in check I sometimes flog them. Somebody dies as a result. Yes, that's true. But the number of the dead is only one-tenth of that killed in road accidents in France on an Easter day. What connection is there between these things? Well, in France there will be more victims on the road next Sunday, whereas here, in my country, there will be fewer thieves....(www.newtimes.ru)

Former President Gnassingbe Eyadema of Togo died only in February 2005. He had seized power in a military coup in 1967, and for 20 years he banned political parties in the country until 1991 when he arranged a flawed election that re-consolidated his stay in power. There were also the duo of Milton Obote and Idi Amin, both of who ruled Uganda consecutively and are believed to have been responsible for the deaths of about one million Ugandans. In addition to his murderous instincts, Idi Amin had a ridiculous and ludicrous obsession for titles, as it is often the case with dictators. He asked to be addressed as "His Excellency, the President for life, Field Marshal, Al Hadji,

19

Dr Idi Amin Dada, Conqueror of the British Empire in Africa". Another dictator was the Democratic Republic of Congo's (former Zaire) President Mobutu Sese Seko, whose personal wealth over-reached that of his country, and he remained in power until he was ousted in 1997. Two other notorious ones have been Ethiopia's Haile Mariam Mengistu, who is said to have been responsible for about 1,500,000 deaths between 1975 and 1979, and Equatorial Guinea's Teodoro Obiang Nguema Mbasogo, who had followed the footsteps of his predecessor, Francisco Macias Nguema, in human rights abuses and manipulation of the electoral process to favour his continuation in office.

Since her independence in 1960 Nigeria has passed through the jackboots of eight military dictators: Major General J.T.U. Aguiyi-Ironsi, General Yakubu Gowon, General Murtala Ramat Mohammed, General Olusegun Obasanjo, Major-General Muhammadu Buhari, General Ibrahim B. Babangida, Generals Sani Abacha and Abdusalami Abubakar. While human rights abuses was a feature of all these regimes, the peak of horror was reached during the reign of General Sani Abacha, a murderous paranoid who blocked his ears against all reasoning. Besides the numerous state-organized bombings and killings, including the horrendous hanging of Nigeria's environmentalist and writer, Ken Saro-Wiwa, and eight of his Ogoni ethnic members on November 10, 1995, it was widely reported that he kept a pond of crocodiles into which he fed some of his perceived opponents. In a characteristic African dictator culture, he was working towards transforming himself into a civilian head of state when he died suddenly in June 1998. Like him, Ahmed Sekou Toure, Kwame Nkrumah, Modibo Keita, Kenneth Kaunda and Milton Obote either died or were overthrown. Three dictators now remain in Francophone Africa. They are Omar Bongo Ondimba of Gabon (now Africa's longest-ruling president), Denis Sassou Nguesso of the Congo Republic and Paul Biya of Cameroon who must only die in office if left alone or be ousted by some violent action.

This criminal betrayal of the African people's pre-independence expectations and the euphoria at independence naturally resulted in the bifurcation of the continent into two. There is the Africa that profits by neo-colonialism and the Africa that struggles to emerge into a free and truly independent post-colonial world. There has also been the Africa of the predator and the Africa of the prey; Africa of the hunter and Africa of the hunted; Africa of the rich and Africa of the poor; Africa of the oppressor and Africa of the oppressed; Africa that is material-driven and Africa that is conscience-governed; and, finally, there is Africa of the farm and Africa of the town. In the last case the farm is his land of birth from which the African empties material resources into the town, the town being his home in Europe or the United States. He flies out from the farm in Africa to a foreign country for the treatment of every headache, and his children must all attend schools abroad. Neo-colonial Africans are usually those who preserve, protect and project the erstwhile colonial master's languages, cultures and literatures. For instance, Ngugi Wa Thiong'o reports that in 1976 he and Seth Adagala, the then director of his play, *The Trial of Dedan Kimathi*, were summoned to Kenya's CID headquarters and warned no longer to interfere with European Theatre [Kenya's National Theatre] (92). Another example is Nigeria's recent addition of French, another European language, to English as a second official language when the nation's indigenous languages are fast losing speakers, especially among the

21

young. Among Nigerian youths today, a disdainful attitude to one's African cultural ways has become a status symbol signifying that one or one's parents have successfully crossed the border from the Africa of the poor to the Africa of the rich. In typical Nigerian lingo, the one "has arrived".

Africa today is therefore one continent only in the physical geographical sense of space. It is, in reality, two continents in one in the sense of its freedom from foreign control, in the standard of living of its peoples, in the physical and social security of its peoples and in the attachment to the continent as a home. The predator-Africa is only physically present on the continent; it is materially, mentally and emotionally in the Diaspora.

Neo-Colonialism and the African Writer

Of the two Africas in this neo-colonial era, the predatory Africa controls most of the media. Hence, much of the time, it is the African rulers' own assessments of their performance that the media would beam to the world irrespective of what numbers succumb daily to poverty, disease, famine and crime; irrespective of the level of insecurity, unemployment and illiteracy in their lands. This partly explains why in Africa the members of the prey-Africa prefer listening to the foreign media because, at least, these ones would report on their condition, although with their usual mockery. Yet, the foreign media are accomplices in this domestication of Western capitalism in Africa, which has left the continent in this laughable stage. Apart from the consistently negative and, perhaps, self-consoling reports showing the poverty of the people and the occasional references to the corruption among the predatory class, these foreign media are elegantly silent about the collusion of western finance institutions and transnational corporations with African dictators to keep the Africans below the economic survival line. While they show on their TV the usual images of sickly and malnourished African children with their distended bellies, of men and women infected with AIDS, and of squalor, they remain calculatingly silent about the poor wages fixed for the African workers by the foreign agencies, about the vaults of western banks distended with the loot from the sweat and blood of African peasants without linking these images to the poor wages, nor the "kwashiokored" children's distended bellies to the distended vaults. As such the localization in Africa of the present economic terrorism goes largely unchecked, is under-reported and hence, under-exposed to the rest of the world.

In the Nigerian situation, for example, this leaves these silent majority with a section of the private press, which often exposes their plight, the Nigeria Labour Congress (NLC), which often protests the frequent increases in the pump price of fuel, and the Academic Staff Union of Universities (ASUU), which has been fighting for the survival of education for even the poor in the country. In the continent as a whole, writers have been in the forefront among cultural producers in the fight for the survival and well being of the prey-Africa. They have fought consistently on the side of the oppressed right from colonial days through the early neo-colonial period till these years of economic globalization. This is a basic role of the modern African writer as it was of his singer-predecessor in the pre-colonial days. This is the role that all major writers and critics in Africa expect of their literature. The slain Ken Saro-Wiwa, perhaps put it most forcefully: "literature must serve society by steeping itself in politics, by intervention, and writers must not merely write to amuse or to take a bemused, critical look at society. They must play an interventionist role" (81). Similarly, Niyi Osundare maintains that a writer in African "is a person that people look up to, in whose work people are trying to see how they relate to the social, cultural and political problems that we are facing in Africa" (Na Allah, 470). The same opinion is articulated by almost every major African writer since Achebe, all of who see the writer as a warrior who should "have an opinion on everything from geography, history, physics, chemistry to the fate of humankind" (Ngugi, 154). Incidentally, even one of Africa's neo-colonial dictators, Guinea's former president Sekou Toure, also stressed this role:

> There is no place outside that fight [African revolution] for the artist or for the intellectual who is not himself concerned with and completely at one with the people in the great battle of Africa and of suffering humanity. (Fanon 166)

This role of being the voice of the voiceless in society has therefore naturally pitted the modern African writer against, first the colonial masters, and now the African proxies of these erstwhile colonialists and, always, with very grave consequences for the writer since, by often suggesting a revolutionary path out of preydom, dictatorial leaders consider literature and its producers a threat. In today's Africa, writers are killed, incarcerated, forced into exile or their works are banned or censored. Above all, there is the inclement publishing climate partly occasioned by the sickly economies and the shift of multinational publishers' interest to the faster-selling school texts. This becomes African governments' 'divine' sluice gate controlling the flow of otherwise "poisonous" material into the public. And so in the end, African writers have ended up suffering "more indignities, threats, humiliations and genuine terror than their counterparts in the rest of the non-western world" (Larson 144).

The frequent incarcerations have resulted in the emergence of a sub-genre of literature on the continent, commonly christened "prison notes." Among those who have contributed to the genre are Wole Soyinka, Ngugi wa Thiong'o, Ken Saro-Wiwa, Lewis Nkosi, Bessie Head, Wahome Murahi, Dennis Brutus, Molefe Pheto, Kofi Awoonor, James Matthews, Todd Matshikiza, Micere Mugo, Percy Mtwa, Luis Bernado Hibwaba and Rene Philombe (Larson 127-128). It is therefore no exaggeration when Josaphat Kubayanda considers African writers as "the new 'nation' of desaparecidos in Africa today" (6), or when Niyi Osundare observes that "Africa today is a dangerous place to think, a risky place to argue" (Omuabor 1). It needs to be stressed, however, that not only writers have been so killed, imprisoned tortured or forced into exile in Africa. In Nigeria, for example, the nation's foremost journalist, Dele Giwa, was killed by a letter bomb on October 19, 1986 while non-writers like Pa Alfred Rewane, Kudirat Abiola, M.K.O. Abiola, Emmanuel Omotehinwa, Shehu Musa Yar' Adua and Obi Wali were also killed during the dark nights of Ibrahim Babangida and Sani Abacha.

The repression has certainly been fossilized in the African literature of the neo-colonial period. While a few of the writers surrendered to the predator African world by either self-censorship or giving up writing altogether (especially in Sierra Leone, Liberia Rwanda, the Congo), others who continued writing have had to inscribe certain strategies into their style. They have had to prefer the passive voice for their sentences, which facilitates the dropping of the actor element (logical subject or agent of the sentence). They also have had to resort to the use of certain symbols: wolves, hyenas, jackals, hangman, bayonets, lions, vultures to represent the predator Africans; and lambs, sheep, skull for the prey (Ushie 355). This, then replicates and reflects the bifurcated structure of the material world of the continent as two Africas in one –the Africa of the predators and the Africa of the prey. This mutual embedding of the realities of the concrete physical world of Africa and the continent's literature into each other also explains the striking similarities in the works of most modern African writers. They all have a common monster to confront: neo-colonialism and Western capitalism. Furthermore, this situation also manifests in literary theorizing in Africa.

The material realities of the continent are yet without those features that could be described as "modern" therefore, "modernism" as a literary theory is not a first-hand experience of the African writer or critique, let alone its successor, "post-Modernism." Since our colonialism is yet to be "posted" anywhere at all, we have reversed from our post-colonial literary journey of the nineteen fifties and the sixties to neo-colonial criticism, which is the major preoccupation of our writers today. The brilliant post-colonialist efforts of the early modern African writers such as Chinua Achebe, Ngugi wa Thiong'O, Kofi Awoonor, Wole Soyinka, Leopold Senghor, Ferdinand Oyono, Mongo Beti, which began with the fictional ridiculing of early converts to western ways, and the work of their coeval critics, were made to reach their menopause soon after their first birth, just like the continent's stillbirth independence.

In Africa and elsewhere in our modern world, the brawn of the transnational corporations and international finance institutions as manifesting in the security personnel of the neo-colonialist nations, their negatively utilized super-brain, which invents ceaselessly more and more confounding economic and financial jargons, and their sheer wealth have combined to dwarf the stature and policing role of the United Nations. The UN has, hence, become nothing more than a Red Cross Society offering first aid to the wounded at the various financial and economic battlefields officially labelled as developing or underdeveloped nations and regions of our worlds. These aids come for the victims of crises and upheavals in Africa, wars and conflicts in Asia's Middle East, terrorism and labour unrests in various parts of the world, and in the form of hunger, disease, illiteracy, poverty and unemployment in many countries.

Conclusion

It is necessary to end this long jeremiad on a note of hope for Africa and humanity by suggesting that African leaders work in close cooperation with their co-wayfarers in the so-called "Third World," and, especially realize that the human resources of any nation are its greatest assets. They must therefore build a bridge between themselves and their intellectuals and cultural producers for the overall health of their countries. No nation rises above the level of its educational development, it is often asserted. Writers and other cultural producers from all over the world must also continue to use their craft for the good of the oppressed peoples of the various lands as their African counterparts have been doing.

Secondly, neo-liberal capitalism, rather than terrorism or racism or religion, constitutes the greatest threat to humankind. Yet, it is a mistake for anyone to think that the brawn and brains and gold of the advanced economies will continue to keep the rest of the world down; or that the ignorance being cultivated in the helpless nations of the world will thrive infinitely; or that their doubles-speak and 'double acts' will continue to be masked to the rest of the world. To think so is to be ignorant of the history of humankind. The only solution is therefore a relatively fair redistribution of wealth such that the poor will not have to be kept awake by hunger, as their being awake will not allow the rich to sleep.

Thirdly the concept of globalization that fosters inter-racial, international, inter-regional and inter-religious understanding and harmony is not evil if it is made to function as a vehicle for spreading the cherished pre-industrial and pre-racialist human values of love, compassion, human solidarity and fellow feeling instead of individualism and cannibalistic materialism. To realize these noble aims of globalization, it would be necessary that an international code of conduct for economic relations among the nations of the world be provided. This should, for example, make it possible and easy for nations to retrieve and return to the source- country all wealth stolen from any part of the world and stored in another. If this were done, it would help Africans much more than the present culture of stuffing the mouths of its dictators with economically poisonous loans.

A happy illustration of the operation of economic globalization is the current fight against corruption in

Nigeria, which is being dictated by the nation's creditor-institutions and nations. The need for this humanistic and healthy form of global co-operation and harmony cannot be more necessary, urgent and crucial than at this time in human history when the human family is being daily faced with natural disasters of all kinds. All these ideas and many other similar positive ones are necessary at this time of our history so that we can return our two Africas to one continent, so that we can return our two worlds to one world, so that we can rehumanise our commodified world by making it conscience-driven rather than gold-governed.

# Nation / Politics

# Chapter 2

## *Defining the Other*

C.Logan

NURRUDIN Farah's *Maps* takes the reader on a journey
into the labyrinth of the mind of a young man, Askar, back
and forth from the time of his birth to the time of his
adulthood in an attempt to find his identity. The novel is set
during the 1969 Somalia-Ethiopia war when Somalia seeks
to reclaim a region populated by Somalis, but which was
given to Ethiopia by the British in 1953. As the borders
move back and forth with the fortunes of war, Askar who
lives in the contested area in his childhood tries to make
sense of his identity as a Somali. His search is further
complicated by the fact that he is raised by an Ethiopian
woman with whom he has a symbiotic relationship and who
is accused of becoming a traitor during the war. The
narrative structure reflects the complexity of the endeavor
as the story is told by three narrators, two of them in a
dialogue from within the self.

We shall examine the dis-location of Askar both within
and without as it probes the borders between the self and
the other, first in a traditional patriarchal society and then in
a country at war. It seeks to show the impossible situation

of the self when national identity and conflict demand that the surrogate mother, experienced as the intimate one, should be redefined as the hated other. It does not solve the riddle of Askar's identity since the author does not, but points out how both the content and the form of the narrative de-construct any attempt to build a watertight definition of identity, ethnic or otherwise, even on the issue of gender. Finally, the aporias of the novel shed some light on the later dissolution of the Somali state and the current presence of Ethiopian troops on Somali soil.

The title of the book *Maps* carries with it the notion of borders and the existence of artificially created spaces where human beings are confined within well delimited territories. But the word 'map' can also suggest other spaces, not defined by geography, but by the interaction of the self with others, and whose intricate design is drawn through the seasons of life and by the unforeseeable fate of relationships. The well acclaimed novel of Nuruddin Farah is certainly all of that and much more. The maps of Nuruddin's novel refer to carved territories on a man-made globe which move with the fortunes of war between Ethiopia and Somalia, but they also denote the natural contour of an Ethiopian surrogate mother's body, where the Somali hero, Askar, is nestled the first years of his life. The challenge of the story is to try to create a neutral space for such a hero whose identity lines are crisscrossed by enemy lines. The narrative attempt to locate a place for him to stand on follows a tortuous path, drawing sometimes contiguous, other times overlapping, but ultimately irreconcilable, maps condemning the narrative to an inconclusive ending which sets it on a Sisyphus-like course of eternal retelling. It is this path and this failed attempt that the present analysis will follow in order to examine the complexity of identity –defined as the differentiation between the self and the other– in the context of one of the post colonial wars on the African continent. But the non completion of the story raises also questions about the relationship between the fictional world within the text, and the material world outside the text. In a novel like *Maps*, where the author defies many of the paradigms of a traditionalist and nationalistic culture, one can raise the question of whether the turbulent political and social realities on the ground can be molded into the author's story, or if the issue of vraissemblance does not lead the narrative in a direction opposed to the one intended by the author. The wrestling involved in the Promethean act of literary creation may also be understood as a struggle between the self and the other.

You and I: dis-location and ambiguity at the onset

*Maps* starts with a declaration of failure, the failure of a hero to find his identity, the failure of the voice of the narrator to circumscribe it, but also the failure of the narrative as an apprenticeship novel or Bildungsroman to come to completion. The hero presented in a beginning – which reads as an ending– has not found his place in society or even resolved the question of meaning. The failure is so great that he does not know who he is, or where he is. It is through the speech of the narrator, addressing the hero with the second person pronoun, that the reader becomes aware of the failure. His voice comes through loud and insistent as the vocative 'you' appears five times in the first paragraph, and follows suit at almost the same rhythm of frequency in the first pages. What the narrator points out to his addressee is his complete sense of disorientation, and his incapacity to locate himself in the world surrounding him. According to the narrator, the addressee is so disconnected with any kind of real space that his lack of anchoring in the 'here' leads him to doubt his own existence, "you wonder if you exist outside of your own thoughts, outside of your own head" (3). Even worse, he cannot be defined by "his community of relations", a term used throughout the novel to describe the extended family. The disappointment of the narrator is evident when he says, "you have become a question to all those who meet you, all those who know you, all those who have any dealings with you" (3). In a culture where the words of Mbiti, "I am because we are; and since we are, therefore I am" (108) have deep resonance, the inability of 'the community of relations' to define the hero speaks of a tragedy from where the self can hardly recover. Anticipating the failed ending that the reader cannot yet understand, the narrative sets out then to tell the story of this aborted quest with the discourse of a second person accusatory narrator.

A vocative 'you', at the beginning of the novel, functions as an authoritarian voice with the right to admonish and reprimand. It occupies a privileged position which sets it above the subsequent voices which will be heard in the narrative and sits in judgment of the validity of the paradigms of the story to come. By taking its distance with the person it addresses, it sets the narrative on a course of dis-connection and deconstruction, acting as a meta-text which in advance is going to discredit the awaited response. The reader is warned not to give credibility to the version of the 'I' narrator, the projected hero, subverting the normal course of the story.

But, the choice of the 'you' at the onset of the novel can also be interpreted as a written transmutation of a traditional Somali genre called "the poetic duel" (29) by John William Johnson. Somali oral literature is famous for its exchange of verses between the gabayaa, (poets) of different clans. They enter into oratorical contests where they not only make a show of their talent but also praise the qualities of their clan so as to celebrate its victories, mock its rivals and respond to accusations of cowardice or to insults. Their primary mode then is the vocative. Nurrudin Farah in his novel *Close Sesame* makes use of one of those poems composed by Mohamed Abdulle Hassan (83). The words of the poems are very harsh, as the composer addresses the defunct general and orders him to tell the story of his defeat to the 'Faithful', on his way to hell. The vocative mode is used throughout the poem, starting in the first verse which addresses Corfield as koofilow, followed by the imperative form of the verb tell (dhedh) twenty two times. It shows clearly that the 'vocative you', and the tone of the harangue of the beginning of the novel fall well within the category of address and dialogic mode that is not just a post-modern dislocation but a familiar Somali way of literary expression.

The message to be conveyed, as the discourse unfolds, is to tell the protagonist, Askar, as he comes to be named, that he should respect, love, and trust Misra, the Ethiopian woman, who raised him although she is accused, as the reader later learns, of betraying 'his people', the Somalis. The urgent plea of the narrator reads as an attempt to contradict the voice who would urge him to do otherwise. It comes as a response, a rebuttal of an argument that has not yet been made, but whose strength the narrator is anxious to deflect before being made. The presence of a rebuttal ahead of the primary argument attests to the narrator's awareness of the strength of the thesis he sets to contradict. What the author is asking his protagonist and his reader, is to believe that an Ethiopian born woman would not betray the Somalis during a war who oppose them to her compatriots. Nuruddin Farah is certainly aware of the formidable objections that his story is going to raise and, as a fine strategist, he attacks his adversaries –Somali tradition and current history– which exist outside the text, before they have a chance to set foot into the narrative. His choice of a dialogical mode of narration between a 'you' narrator and an 'I' narrator indicates the challenges that the story will face as it develops. Their dialogue can be interpreted as an argumentation between two points of view, the author (the you) and nationalistic sentiment (the I), outside the text, rather than a simple post-modern dialogue between a narrator and a protagonist.

Misra and Askar as 'I and thou' relationship

The author faces the challenge at hand, by having the hero, Askar, stripped as much as possible of his 'Somaliness' in the creation of the circumstances of his birth and his early childhood story. The text is built as variations on one central theme: the foundation of Askar's existence is in Misra, the surrogate Ethiopian mother. Not only does he owe his life to her, since she found him by the dead body of his mother and therefore saved him from certain death, but his coming into 'being' is intimately linked to his relationship with her. Misra and Askar's relation is described as a type of 'I and thou' relationship, where the self owes its ontological existence to the 'thou' that it relates to: "[m]an first becomes an I through a You" (80). It builds their relationship on an impregnable fortress against which no other secondary identity markers, such as ethnicity, religion or citizenship, can prevail. To make the case even more convincing, the author creates a child who was as much responsible for establishing the relationship as Misra. The narrator reminds the protagonist, that he, himself, refused to recognize the "thou" of the tradition, 'the community of relations' as his extended family is called.

> The community of relations decided that Misra, the woman who was once a servant, would 'mother you'. One thing ought to be said here- you were the one who made the choice, the community of relations had to approve of; you were barely a week old. And Misra agrees with this statement. So, begrudgingly, would Uncle Qorrax in Kallafo. (5)

The author bestows on Misra a variety of attributes which qualify her as the mother of Askar. She is, says the narrator, "maternal like the cosmos. . . giving, giving"(6) and even on a stronger mode, "to you she was the cosmos" (6). Misra comes also as close as possible to being an actual mother, by giving him back his life, which can be called a rebirth. His previous ephemeral birth experience was linked with death, the death of his mother, but also the death that the trace of fingers around his neck suggests –the death that may be his mother tried to inflict upon him (4). The 'you' narrator states :

> She was the one that took you away from 'yourself', as it were, she was the one who took you back form the world of the womb and innocence, and washed you clean in the water of a new life and a new

christening, to produce in you the corrected etches of a young self, with no pained memories, replacing your missing parents with her abundant self which she offered generously to you-her new discovered child! and you? (6)

The map of the first years of life of Askar can be drawn around the body of Misra as the narrator insists on their physical closeness "by tucking you between her breasts...and she smelled of your urine precisely the same way you smelled of her sweat" (9). His sharing her bed sets him between her and her lover, Aw-Adan, which leads him to say "to you, said Aw-Adan, she was your space" (11). The 'I' narrator draws the same map around them, and does not challenge the thesis of the 'you' narrator. He agrees that she gave him life, "from the instant she lifted me....I was a living human being and I began to exist" (24). He talks about the physical closeness he felt, adding that he was Misra's "third breast" (24) and later "third leg" (75). He confirms that he hated Uncle Qorrax, the patriarchal representative of the Somali tradition, by telling the story of his failed visit a few days after his birth. (28). He also widens the map of Misra's body to include the room within the compound that she shared with him and puts everybody else in the world of the 'other'. "My uncle "says Askar, "decided to earmark a fenced mud with its separate entrance for our own use...We had a life to live and a compound which was all our own Misra and I" (28). Askar is not within 'the community of relations' but on the edge of it, looking on as a mere observer. He says clearly that he establishes his own territory "the freehold kingdom of which I was the undisputed Lord. Since I held Uncle Qorrax his wives and his children in total awe and at bay it appeared there were only Misra and Karin whose civilized company I kept" (29). He also calls Misra 'mother' but not in front of his relatives who frown on his use of the appellation (25). Even more significantly, Askar says that Misra and he shared secrets (39) establishing a very strong bond whose cultural importance is emphasized by the fact that Nuruddin Farah, made of 'secrets', the theme and the title of a later novel.

Both the 'you' and the 'I' narrators who are engaged in a dialog of sorts, in spite of their disagreements on other issues, concur on this thesis: Askar owes his life and his coming into 'being' to Misra; she is an inescapable part of who he is; they lived for many years inside of the same map and the traditional Somali 'community of relations' stands outside of that map. For the early childhood years of his hero, the author has been able to create a place where he and Misra can stand together, challenging "the other" of the Somali tradition, keeping them from interfering with their relationship or putting it into jeopardy.

Yet, even the accusing voice of the second-person narrator, in spite of all its efforts to show that Askar belongs to Misra and to Misra only, and that they exist in the tight reciprocal embrace of an I-thou relationship, does not completely succeed in claiming Misra's exclusive ownership of Askar. There are in the text disclaimers of the thesis presented in the first chapters. A closer look reveals that Askar's choosing and acceptance of Misra is not immediate, "you would shun and withdraw any contact"(5). It seems like it was the water that she bathed him in, that calmed him and acted as a medium between him and her, not the fresh blood of a woman who gives birth. The metaphor of baptism the author uses to speak of Askar's rebirth, with the term "christening" (6) reinforces the importance of water. Moreover, the use of a term which comes from the Christian lexicon and which seems incongruous in a Muslim milieu, serves to underline another dimension of the otherness of Misra, religious affiliation. Although, there is no inkling that Misra would be Christian, Ethiopians are often contrasted with the Somali because of their belonging to one of the oldest Christian church: the Coptic church. The wars between Somalis and Ethiopians have often been interpreted as religious wars, by both Somali and Europeans, from the time of Ahmed Gurey (the left handed) in the 16th to the most recent episode with the Islamic court in 2007. Although Nurrudin Farah tries to stay away from religious parameters, his vocabulary betrays an underlying reality which often draws stronger lines of separation than nationalistic claims.

Another episode also, challenges the claim of Misra, as the only valid mother. The narrator informs the reader that in spite of Misra's attempt to nurse Askar, he refuses stubbornly (8). Her interpretation of Askar's refusal is that his mother, Arla, had a chance to nurse him, before she died, acknowledging the claim of another woman, to Askar's maternal rights. Actually, Misra does not deny Askar's connection with his natural mother nor his origins: she is even the one who whispers to him secrets about his father and mother's manner of death, when his own relatives do not dare talking about it. The narrator, when he addresses Askar with the vocative 'you', is the one who insists otherwise. The narration within the narrator's discourse, on the other hand, gives a lot of factual information about Askar's birth, even Misra' s acceptance of his 'Somaliness', which points in another direction. Even the strong voice of the 'you' narrator cannot build an air-tight argument about the Askar's appartenance, which makes the argument sound more as a plea than the enunciation of an irrefutable truth.

The gap introduced by the narration is retaken and dwelt on by Askar. He constantly goes back to what the 'you' narrator wants him and the reader to forget: there is a before Misra, and the before matters. He is also obsessed by his manner of birth, wondering if he has killed his mother, to the point that Misra made the subject become taboo in their household (30). His fixation with his mother's death even takes him into very dangerous territory, when he tells Misra that he wants to kill her. To her startled reaction he replies "so you would be a corpse like my mother" and he gives as explanation "only in death could she and I be united -only in death, her death, could she and I be related, only then would I somehow feel as though we were a mother and a son" (37). His intent then, was to draw closer to her, but it certainly anticipates the later development as he remembers his words now that he is 17, and that, because Misra has been accused of betrayal "he has a good reason to do it" (57).

Askar goes back and forth constantly between those two 'truths'– he is Misra's, which the text claims – and the other, that places him in the reality of historical events outside the text: he is the son of a Somali mother who died at birth and whose father was an enemy of the Ethiopians who caused his death. He is then part of a Somali community who looks at him with awe because of the history and the past he carries on his shoulders as the orphan of a Somali patriot. Those realities place him into a map other than Misra's bodily contour and set him inside nationalistic borders, where she is 'the other'. The territoriality issues that exist outside the text cannot be forgotten. No, Askar has not been completely re-birthed; no his memories have not been completely erased; no the 'you' narrator cannot ignore the fundamental dis-location of his self at birth. His position is very precarious. The story of Askar's birth draws two different maps around him, and one map cannot overwrite the other: no palimpseste. Askar is condemned to a constant balancing act by his creator. He is right to exclaim "who I am, where I am" (93) at every turn of the narrative.

Tradition as an assault against the 'I and thou' relationship

As the plot develops, the first frontal assault into the relationship between Misra and Askar is his going to Koranic school. The words of Askar's paternal uncle Qorrax are clear enough when he introduces him to the Koranic teacher:

> I bring to you this blessed morning, my brother's only son whose name is Askar. Like all human beings, Askar is part bone and part flesh. The flesh is yours and you may punish it. The bones however are ours, by which I mean the family –and you may not harm them unnecessarily. Do you accept Askar as your pupil as you have accepted before him my own sons of my own body and blood? (81)

All the weight of tradition is expressed in these words: Askar does not belong to Misra. Uncle Qorrax reclaims his dominion over him as a male and a blood relative. He explains further also, why Askar who is only five years old, is to be taken to the school: "For there is no man in the compound in which he lives and one may take boys away from the bad influence of women" (81). The statement is

42

clear: the purpose of sending boys to Koranic school is to separate them from their mother and introduce them to a man's world. The move is not anti-Ethiopian as such, but simply the reflection of the prejudices of a patriarchal society about women. The new map drawn around Askar sets Misra clearly as an outside 'other', but this time because of her gender. In order to offset the weight of tradition represented in this statement, Nurrudin Farah will have to create another uncle, a maternal one this time, whose personality will be at the opposite side of the spectrum. Yet his sending to the Koranic school does not succeed in separating Askar from Misra. Misra, aware of the traditions and respectful of them accepts the new situation and encourages him to learn. Askar is the one who finds the separation painful (76), especially because of the harshness of the teacher, Aw-Adan, who also happens to be Misra's lover. But when Misra decides to help him "God became fun" (77) says Askar.

The second ritual, the circumcision, has greater implications. This important rite of passage from childhood to adulthood which resets the novel in the context of a Bildungsroman, can be found in many autobiographies of African writers. *L'enfant noir* Camara Laye (1954), or *L'aventure ambigue* Cheik Amadou Kane (1961) give great details on this rite of passage, particularly trying to explain, to the often scandalized western reader, how the suffering caused by male circumcision has a validity of its own. Nevertheless its occurrence does not necessarily subvert the premises of the relationship between Misra and Askar as mother and son. It parallels the necessary cutting of the umbilical chord or of the oedipal knot, if one wants to use Freudian paradigms. Yet, because the relationship between Misra and Askar is so much based on physical closeness, it is not surprising that it would have a strong impact on their relationship and redraw the borders of Askar's self. It is still a dis-location of another kind than his birth, and may be a necessary or healthy dislocation, but a dislocation all the same. In the words of Askar "During my brief sojourn in the life of pain two things occurred: one I lost myself in ité two, I took a hold of a different 'self' one that had no room and no space for Misra" (92). The nightmare that he recalls shortly after this separation, signals how traumatic the separation was "Who am I who am I, where am I? where am I? Who am I? Misra was not there, I was alone. And no one told me where I was, no one told me who I was" (93). The territory he used to stand on has disappeared, putting in jeopardy his identity: he cannot be defined by Misra anymore. The following chapter informs us that Somalia has become "Mother " (97) and has replaced Misra, setting him on a colliding course with her.

War and Devastation: the 'thou' becomes the 'other'

When one chooses a country to become 'mother', a declaration of war has very serious implications. The war with Ethiopia which starts as he is still recovering from the 'land of suffering ' precipitates his passage into adulthood. All of a sudden everything accelerates, all the paradigms change; what was presented as secondary, becomes primary; what was innocuous, dangerous; the casual facts told in the narration about his origins come to the forefront of the narrative. The 'I 'narrator is suddenly aware of their differences and he "remember[s] that she was different from us, she was not a Somali like me and the others ;" (94) He finds her 'ugly' and has ceased to share his secrets with her.

They are entering into the inferno of Manichaeism where it is 'them against us', 'my people' versus 'their people'. They bear now the name of 'enemy' the most dangerous definition of the 'other' because it puts them on opposite side of the new dividing lines. Misra, who knows what war is about, anticipates the destruction of their relationship when she tells him that her people will kill him if he accompanies her to her village "They will kill you. My people will kill you" (95). Then she adds, to a startled Askar, giving the 'coup de grace' to the relationship and anticipating the ending of the novel that 'his people', or even he, might kill her. "Kill...Yes. Kill. Loot. Rape. Murder. In the name of your people. "One day I might kill you?" he asks. "May be," she said and walked out of the room" (95). Could Nurudin Farah have avoided to put Misra and Askar in a war setting where they became each other's enemy? Could he have ignored the real wars on the ground in his imaginary world, the world of literary fiction?

Hilaal as the attempt to restore the place of the 'other'

Nurruddin Farah nevertheless, even in the midst of war, does not give up trying to make the relationship work. The narrative in the second part of the novel can be read as an attempt to counter the destructive effects of the war and to restore some grace to the Misra-Askar relation. In a paradoxical move, he removes Askar physically from the presence of Misra, taking him away from the theatre of war, but at the same time creates another character, which already has appeared in the narrative, uncle Hilaal and whose main role is going to be to renew the ties between Askar and Misra, by being Misra's advocate.

To introduce this new character more thoroughly, the author goes back to the 'you' narrator of the beginning of the novel. But the voice of the 'you' in chapter 7, adopts a different tone from the one of the first chapter. The mode is not accusatory but explanatory. There is no repetition of a vocative 'you' who accuses the protagonist, but a voice who tries to help him sort out events in a new world, totally unfamiliar to him. It is still the authorized voice who holds the truth about Askar, but its mood is different. One has the impression that it is the voice of uncle Hilaal himself which is behind the second person pronoun. The protean character of the you, with its shifting persona, allows the narrative to enter into a different mode, and prepares the reader for the discourse of an 'interpreter'.

Uncle Hilaal is presented as standing in clear contrast with Uncle Qorrax. The narrator uses the phrase "on the other hand" (17) when he is first mentioned in the narrative. He lives in the capital city of Mogadiscio which is described as having: "a multi cultural, multiracial heritage" (158). So although it is politically speaking more 'Somali' than Kallafo which is within the Ethiopian border, it is presented as a place of diversity and modernity. Uncle Hilaal's home itself reflects additional differences: it is a house where there is electricity, running water and many mirrors (a novelty for Askar ) and where only he and his wife live. Askar actually admits missing the atmosphere of the compound when he first arrived: "you were sad, you said, because they did not have 'a festivity of going-on'. . . and where one felt one was a member of a community" (144).

Uncle Hilaal is highly educated and teaches at the university. When it comes to religion, there is no hint of any religious feeling from his part. He talks about religion the

46

same way he talks about philosophy or politics without giving us any inkling of what he believes. Although he does not live within "the Somali cosmos" being Somali is of utmost importance to him and he goes to great lengths to explain to Askar the specificity of its culture. He revels in the world of ideas and intellectual argumentation. But what sets him apart from Somali tradition is that he has one wife and no children. The latter especially is very surprising in a society where having descendants is of utmost importance. This is where the creation of the character seems very deliberate: he transgresses all the limits of a Somali patriarchal culture and his explanation about his vasectomy stretches the limit of the vraissemblable. Aware of the vraisemblance the case, the author introduces a defense of the validity of his character by the character itself. He admits that

> Society does not approve of a man who loves a woman who does not bear him children a woman who does not cook his food. . . to our society this is unpardonable. . . This is why you don't see many people, coming to, and going away, from our house. My relations have boycotted me. (144)

The transgression of uncle Hilaal's society boundaries is also exemplified in his feminine qualities. It is he, a male, who reminds Askar of Misra, "physically, Uncle Hilaal was the replica of Misra- only he was a man- which at this point of time did not make any difference anyway"(135). The author insists by specifying that the resemblance has to do with physical features "It was Hillal who reminded you of Misra -he was the natural body odor. And he was fatter and liked to make bodily contact- just like Misra!" Besides,

47

his doing the cooking puts him in the "contradictory role of 'Mother'" (18). The author goes even further in transgressing the limits of the environing culture, or of any culture for that matter, by describing uncle Hilaal, when in a state of depression as "Misra in season," euphemism used to describe the time of menstruation. The transgression of the male/female divide had appeared in the first part of the novel, when Askar mentions to Misra that he discovered blood on his groin:

> The following morning, he awoke and was confronted with an inexplicable mystery: there was blood on the sheet he had covered himself with, blood under him too. Most specifically, there was blood on his groin. He sought Misra's response.
> "You've begun to menstruate she said looking at him with intense seriousness (...) "He said, 'But I am a man. How can I menstruate? (105)

She does not seem surprised by this event out of the ordinary and a few lines later "he reminded her of a conversation they had a few days before that he envied women their monthly periods" (105). The issue is certainly complex and the meaning ambiguous, as the statement from Askar, that he envied women their 'monthly periods' suggests. Certainly, not forgetting that the author is a male writer, one cannot help wondering how the lengthy details that the author gives of Misra's menstruation, in the first part of the book (48-49), might not come from a fascination of a male subject for something that he cannot experience; something he tries to understand but still remain a mystery to him –a mystery he wants to enter as a violation of a woman private space. The fascination for women's menstruation appears in another novel of Nuruddin Farah, Secrets. The protagonist, as a young boy decides to taste the menstruation blood of an older girl, Sholoongo. The choice of a young boy, in both cases, to express that fascination makes it more innocuous, and one wonders if this might not be the limit of Nuruddin Farah's feminist stance.

The desire to trespass the female divide seems to be the author's, and not Askar's. In the conversation which follows Askar's discovery of blood, he denies strongly wanting to be a woman (he would rather be sick) (107). The reaction of Uncle Hilaal, when later on, Askar again has an experience of menstruation points in the same direction. He is so disturbed and shaken that he goes to the garden and burns all of his paper and pronounces this sentence that Askar repeats "wars are river who burn" (152) being at a complete loss in front of that phenomenon. Menstruation seems an ultimate frontier that the male writer cannot cross.

Uncle Hilaal's aporia

Although Uncle Hilaal, in his feminist rhetoric and his transgressing of the male and female boundaries, stretches the limits of the vraissemblable in the narrative, he stays very much within conventional parameters when it comes to his ideas about Somali identity, relocating the narrative well within the historical reality outside the text. Although it is not, the ideas of the patriarchal and pastoral society that he presents, where genealogies, clan and religion are the main markers, the identity discourse he pronounces is very representative of the ideas of the Somali intelligentsia before and after Independence.

49

Those ideas were built around two main axes: uniqueness and homogeneity. The claim of the Somalis is that they were unique in Africa because they were homogeneous, contrary to many other African states, especially their neighbors, Ethiopia and Kenya. The national dream of the founders of the new Republic of Somalia was to create a state which included all the regions where Somali speaking people lived. The novel presents briefly the issue through Karin's husband, who was an admirer of Ernest Bevin, a British diplomat, who advocated the reunification of all the Somali speaking countries (73) after the second war, as the Europeans were trying to redraw the maps in Africa.

Those regions altogether were five and came to be represented by the five points of the star on the Somali flag: the North under British rule, the South under Italian rule, the Ogaden which had been under British protectorate but was given to Ethiopia in 1953, Djibouti under French rule, and the Northern Frontier District given to Kenya by the British in 1963. The two first regions had become one to form the new Independent State of Somalia, and one of the goals of the new Republic was to bring the other three regions, under Somali rule. Since the countries that held them, were not willing to give them up, warfare of one type of the other came to be seen as the way to accomplish that goal. Insurgent movements, such as "The Somali Western Liberation Movement," to which Askar's father belonged, flourished in those regions. For this reason the concept of homogeneity led to a nationalist stance which implicitly justified armed struggle. Therefore Uncle Hilaal, when he tries to explain to Askar what it means to be Somali, enters into a very treacherous territory, steeped with nationalistic feelings, and territorial claims. Yet what makes the operation hazardous for Uncle Hilaal, Misra's advocate, is that sooner or later the issue of where Misra fits, will have to be undertaken. How can he define Somali identity without putting Misra in the category of 'the other'? In many ways, his declarations about Somali identity are going to be within the same parameters as his contemporaries: they are a people "who share a common ancestor and who speak the same language" (147). He also uses the same terminology when he speaks of "cultural homogeneity" (148). Nevertheless, he tries to stay clear of other markers, such as religion, which is still keeping in pace with the religious skepticism of many of the intellectual Somalis in the sixties and the seventies. But it becomes more perilous when he tackles the issue of "ethnicity." On one hand, he says that "there is no ethnic difference which sets apart the Somali from the Ethiopian" (167) yet he uses the terminology when describing the Somali elsewhere in the text. "Every ethnic Somali is entitled to live in the Somali Republic. They may belong to any Somali-speaking territory, be it Kenyan, Ethiopian or even Djebouti" (156). He tries to find a way out of the thorny issue by making the language, the centerpiece of Somali identity. Uncle Hilaal states that even Misra could be Somali since she spoke the language well enough the language (167). Yet even this definition has its own pitfalls as one can argue that they are varieties of the Somali language and language can be also used for a politic of exclusion.

The aporia of Uncle Hilaal's discourse comes from the difficulty to define the concept of identity itself. As the Anthropologist Jean Francois Gossiaux says rightly "la question de l'identité n'est pas "qui suis-je? "mais qui je suis par rapport aux autres, [the question of identity is not who am I? but who I am in comparison with the others]" (2).

51

The best way to describe the Somali is by contrasting them with the Ethiopians, which is illustrated by the fact that his explanations about Somali identity, come after Askar asks "Who is an Ethiopian?" (147). Misra, then cannot be both Ethiopian and Somali, she has to choose; the only way she can cease to be the 'other' is to become Somali. Uncle Hilaal's solution is reminiscent of the French colonial politics of "assimilation". It makes a way for her to be inside of the Somali map, but then she needs to renounce her own identity: no diversity here.

Historically speaking, it took the dissolution of the Somali state for the Somali intellectuals to question the homogeneity stance. Ali Jimale Ahmed, in 1995, finally spoke of a 'myth of identity' created by the regime of Syad Barre "The states' own charlatan produced their own version of a stable, contradiction free society, marked by complete homogeneity" (8). Now the identity discourse has come to terms with the current terminology of social sciences, the same way the concept of homogeneity echoed the European categories of nationhood in the 1950's as stated by Michel Walzer (2). The homogeneity discourse had put Somalia on an equalitarian foot with European nation and allowed it to make its territorial claims. The character of uncle Hilaal who, otherwise, has been able to defy all of the Somali paradigms, is caught in the inextricable politics of identity, in the world of reality which puts Misra outside the map, notwithstanding the efforts of the author, to bring her in.

Askar as the Other

It is an interesting aspect of the structure of the narrative, that the one who challenges the conventional paradigms of the new Somali identity would be Askar. He changes role and unmasks the inconsistencies of Uncle Hilaal, or rather deconstructs the modern Somali identity that Uncle Hilaal, and the intelligentsia, had painstakingly elaborated. The episode of the "carta d'identitá" illustrates magnificently the point.

For its acquisition, Askar goes through a process that seems as much a rite of passage as going to Koranic school. Askar talks about "the fuss" which was made about the clothes he was to wear on the day his picture was taken, and he describes the excitement of Uncle Hillal on the day he received the card in the mail:" He walked in exalted, like a man who has discovered a most coveted treasure all by himself" (163). At first, Askar does not understand his excitement for "a paper whose green, had faded a little" (164) and was "cheaply printed" (164) but as solemnly as Uncle Qorrax entrusted him to the care of Aw-Adan in Koranic school, Uncle Hillal entrusts the 'carta d'identitá to Askar himself

> From the way he gave to me, you would have thought he was entrusting me a brand new life'. are , he seemed to say with another life all your own....While I was looking at it, Uncle Hillal engaged Salaado in a solemn conversation, as if she were to be a witness at my being wed to myself." (163)

This card represents the new identity created for Askar by Uncle Hilaal; it is an identity according to the new way of being Somali; an identity which means citizenship; an identity of a "mother tongue" written down; an identity which is Western enough to be called by a foreign word "carta d'identitá"; an identity which is individual and does not include "the community of relations". Askar is puzzled by this new concept of identity: "How passport-size photographs would help anybody identify a person?"(165) he wonders.

A few days before he had received his card, he asked a question that upset Uncle Hilaal greatly "And I see that in identity papers there is a place allotted to biological parents and to guardians but none to somebody like Misra"(162). Uncle Hilaal did not miss the meaning of that remark. He who seems to have all the answers is at a loss. He appears so "dejected" that Askar promises himself: "I would never raise the subject again"(162) He tries to accept his new identity the best he can "But I confess, I did think that I was expected to perceive from that moment onwards, to perceive myself in the identity created for me" (165).

Askar, in this episode, deconstructs the new identity which is created for him and all of the Somalis who live outside of the urban centers of Somalia, but most especially outside of Mogadiscio, the capital city, the seat of the government. Askar resists this new identity where the written Somali has become normative; where it is a taboo to talk about one's clan; where secular knowledge replaces religious knowledge; where there is no mention of circumcision or polygamy. The dislocation of the self is not anymore from the separation of the natural mother who dies, it is between competitive maps of Somali identity. In the map of the new 'modern' Somali identity, Askar is the 'other', the foreigner, who cannot fit, or is it them, the creators of this new Somalia, who are the foreigners?

In a later book *Secrets* (1998), after eight years of an interminable civil war, Nurudddin Farah brings to the forefront a hidden Somali identity of magic and taboo, through the intriguing character of the woman Sholoongo who is called "a classical other"(191). In a much more dramatic way that Askar, she helps unmask what is behind the smooth definition of a homogeneous identity that Uncle Hilaal had tried to clothe Askar with. Nonno, the grandfather of the main character, Kalaman, says of her:

> I think of her as the shaman who has come not to heal but to dispossess us of our secret wills. I compare her, wrongheadedly to one's idea of the clan: a notion difficult to locate, slippery, contradictory, testing one's capacity to remain patient during one's trying times. (295)

The resistance of the character Askar, to the molding of his uncle Hilaal, brings to mind the appearance in the street of Mogadicio in 1991, of the so-called mooreyan , who answering the call of their clan elders, came to loot, rape, and destroy the space of the new Somalia which was being constructed around Mogadiscio. One cannot but marvel at the realism of Nuruddin Farah, who in the middle of this imaginary tale, has inserted the Askars of Somalia whose behavior is as unpredictable as the one in the fiction. But even more, the irreconcilable Ethiopian Somali relationship, in spite of the efforts of an uncle Hilaal, should inform the International community that Ethiopian troops cannot establish a credible Somali government. Unfortunately, as it was in the sixties, where the ideological wars between the United States and its rival, the Soviet Union were fought on the African continent, 'terrorism' now has overshadowed any intelligent or intelligible politics of the Western powers. "The Clash of Civilization" (Huntington 1996) which is played out on Somali territory, re-awakens the religious interpretation of the conflicts between the two neighboring countries. However, the Ethiopian-Somali issue is not the only one which is impeding a resolution of the conflict; the issue of borders, in the present situation, has become of foremost importance. If Askar were looking at the map of Somalia today, he would have a hard time following the different lines which are being drawn or redrawn. Where are the boundaries and who decides where they are? Is it the warlords and their militia? Is it the people of the new (or not so new anymore) but self proclaimed Somaliland Republic? Or is it the people of Puntland? Where are the Somali? Who are the Somali?

Who is the self and who is the other?

The third part of the narrative does not bring anything new in the overall design of the novel but the ritual murder of Misra reshuffles again, all its different parts, leading them to their inevitable confrontation and their failed resolution: Askar's inability to mature; the impossible reconciliation of his different selves; the indecision of the ending. It brings two of the underlying maps of the narrative to a stalemate: the imaginary territory of the literary text, and the indomitable territory of reality. This leads us to restate our original thesis: the dislocation of the self in *Maps* may not be after all, something which happens to Askar, the failed hero of the apprenticeship novel, but rather something which happens to the author both within and without the act of writing. Derrida talks about writing as "une descente hors de soi, [a descent outside of one self] which reveals to the author "l'autre fraternel,[the fraternal other]" (19) making the dislocation of the self at the heart of literary creation. Except that the dislocation of an African writer might not be located at the same place as the one of a post-modern European writer: for the latter it happens, within the self, for the first within and without the reality of war; the actual redrawing of political maps, in peace conferences or other international venues; the flesh and bone refugees who wander around the country side; the exiles dispersed to the four corners of the world; all, and more are dislocations which do not come from within but from without. The writer, –whether or not a political activist – cannot distance himself from his links to a real territory of suffering and destruction. The added dislocation of writing in a language which is not the mother-tongue, so central to the understanding of identity, puts him at the center of otherness, as a foreigner in both the land of the real and the land of fiction. How can one know then, who is the other and who is the self?

# Chapter 3

## *The Chattering, and Hope*

O.Akinola

LITERARY contextualism advocates that texts can be interpreted only when they are placed against the backgrounds from which they emanate. Contextualism does not necessarily cut off the literary work or hinder us from using our knowledge of other disciplines to understand what happens. In fact, what is fundamental to contextualism is a recognition that, although literature refers to the real world outside of us, it nevertheless creates a world in which these images and feelings are seen outside of the familiar categories; they are defamiliarized by the structure of the work so that we can see these images and objects in a new distinctive light. This paper therefore investigates the controversy about the relational quality and dependent nature of text on the context and the exigency that inform the deliberate distortions of certain figures and images by contemporary African playwrights.

Every African writer is obsessed with the problem of creating an image (positive or negative) to suit a vision, belief, ideology, tribe, sex or environment. Images are not directly responsible for reality or context; quite the opposite is true because certain images –social (sex, marriage, violence), economic or political permeate most African Writings as experienced from reality or context of writing. African writers are uncertain whether to confine themselves within the European frame of reference or to create new and opposing images or contexts perhaps designed on traditional values rather than the negative and stereotyped views that are profoundly ingrained in the works of African playwrights particularly the home video industry.

This emphasis is important because images are especially vital cultural products, for they reflect given socio-political contexts and offer retrospective accounts of traditions, behavioural norms and aesthetic values. It is therefore essential that a writer must have the vision to perceive life's multiple dimensions, particularly as played in his own society or context in which he lives, without undue recourse to external influence. In Nigeria, there has been a symbiotic relationship between drama and politics, since art is the handmaiden of politics in any society. The imaginative power and perception of an artist are not conceived in an abstract mechanistic society, hence he writes within the ambience of a human society.

Ngugi argues that an artist's work therefore, becomes a reflection of that society economic structure, its class formation, its conflicts and contradictions, its class, power, political and cultural struggles. Nigerian playwrights incorporate political themes and ideology in their play as Achebe rightly points out that any African creative writer who tries to avoid the big social and political issues of contemporary Africa will end up being completely irrelevant like that absurd man in the proverb who leaves his house burning to pursue a rat fleeing from the flame. This informs the position of Nigerian playwrights who reacted to the political problems in their societies both during the colonial and postcolonial periods. This growing sense of political awareness manifested itself in Soyinka's satirical sketches and revues in a collection titled Before the Black out and later in a full length play, *Kongi's Harvest*. According to Gbilekaa, both the revues and Kongi's Harvest were an attack on power, arrogance, megalomania and corruption, the handicap or lack of a progressive political vision that characterized politics in Nigeria's First Republic.

This relationship between drama and politics is based on the fact that a dramatist should not only be an entertainer but a teacher of moral values and a special adviser on political matters. Augustos Boal corroborates this argument in a way that demonstrates clearly Aristotle's description of politics as a social relationship. "All theatre is necessarily political", he argues, "because all the activities of man are political and theatre is one of them. Those who try to separate theatre from politics try to lead us into error and this is a political attitude" (9). This is further established by Ngugi Wa Thiong'o, who sees it from the point of view of the imperialist domination of African cultures, literature, song and dance1: "Every writer is a writer in politics. The only question is what and whose politics" (Preface).

Herbert Ogunde in the colonial era used his theatre to challenge the colonial government for the repressive manners in which Nigerian affairs were being conducted. His was a political tool in the quest for Nigeria's independence, for which commitment, Michael Etherton observes, "specifically saw his company as the means by which he could help establish the cultural independence of the Africans in Nigeria as a back-up for the growing movement for political and economic independence..." (45).

Ogunde however, was not indifferent to the political problems during the postcolonial era, which led to violence and avarice. Ogunde lampooned the attitude of the political leaders who fought one another using various dangerous means to achieve their goals[2]. He then produced plays like "Yoruba Ronu" and "Otito Koro" as a reaction to this political logjam in his immediate environment.

The decline in the relevance of dramatists like Ogunde and Duro Ladipo came about due to the persistent need to address more national problems, which demand a national or more acceptable medium of expression. Hence the theatre of English expression was born. This theatre tradition is unique because, while the early dramatists used the local languages, English language was its own medium of expression. Secondly, while indigenous theatre is rooted in the people's culture, and the state of development among them before and after their encounter with the colonial masters, the theatre of English expression developed as a product of the influence of Euro-American culture on Nigerian culture.

There are two categories of playwrights in the theatre of English expression: the pioneer group who wrote with the aim of recreating history and also asserting their cultural position here the works of Wale Ogunyemi, Wole Soyinka, J.P. Clark, Ola Rotimi and Zulu Sofola are prominent. In the second category are those whose plays show a lot of agitation and protest against the status quo. Foregrounding this movement are the works of Osofisan, Sowande, Omotosho, lately Ola Rotimi (in his plays *If and Hopes of the Living Dead*) and a host of current Nigerian playwrights.

Osofisan in his bid to project his ideology reconstructs history and this is clearly shown in *The Chattering and the Song*, when the character of Alafin Abiodun who, in the history of Oyo is regarded as a benevolent ruler, is presented in *The Chattering and the Song* as a tyrant. The playwright uses Latoye to question the oppressive nature of the feudal past showing us the parallel between the past and the present. This conclusion is authentic because it was first staged during the regime of General Gowon who had installed himself through a coup-d'etat, and his government was very oppressive and decadent nature of his rule was an eye sore to the generality of the people. The play builds a link between a modern military "monarch" and a past feudal parallel in which individual kings manipulated and lorded it over their subjects, in order to keep perpetually in power[3].

Generally, Gowon's reign marked a corresponding increase in crime, corruption, injustice, oppression and social decadence. For contemporary playwrights like Ola Rotimi and Femi Osofisan, this state of crisis offered them not only the opportunity to question the whole socio-economic structure, operated in Nigeria, but also to examine urgent social problems like the armed robbery phenomenon in Osofisan's *Once Upon Four Robbers*, student violence in Sowande's *The Night Before* and the obscenity of undistributed property in Omotosho's *The Curse*.

These new playwrights adopt a socio-historical context in examining events in their society by going to the roots in order to establish causative factors before prescribing appropriate solutions to the problems. They differ remarkably from the first generation of playwrights in the sense that their plays advocate fundamental reforms of the political and economic structures of their society.

Osofisan believes that writers must "sow regenerative seeds in the community's flesh" and he is against a writer merely reflecting the sorrow and incoherence present in an oppressive society. *The Chattering and the Song* illustrates the obligation on playwrights and intellectuals to use their intellect and their privileged position towards a critical analysis and positive reconstruction of their society by a collective commonwealth. According to Femi Fatoba who says the use of "Iwori otura" from the literary corpus of Ifa poetry is the metaphor for the above conclusion"4.

> Funlola: Say there's famine: Iwori otura…
> Leje:   You're searching for food, you're thirsty and dry… in your searching and thirsting, I come across you; I am the tortoise, The great traveller…
> Funlola: Please mister tortoise, my life's in your hands: Iwori otura: you've travelled the world lead me into safety to fertile lands…  And climb on my back: I've travelled the world, 1 know them all, those fertile lands…
> Funlola: Dancing together, in the loom of the state: Iwori Otura…. (55)

It is noteworthy from the playwright's ideological stand point that the character, through simile, state their pitiable social position and how from that position of being "just like a thread", they move in unity, to a position of strength where the thread, working with and in the protective and guiding functions of the shuttle, became the foundation of a protective and decorative national symbol.

There is a marriage of revolutionary ideals as symbolized by the many and positive characteristics of weaver-birds which is the main thrust of the play, and in the narration of Iwori otura, and Keke, the man questioned Olomijo, the woman. Sontri leads with the riddle and being a master riddler wins Yajin, for which his conscience pricks him. From that point on, "a bigger riddle begins," because Yajin was until then engaged to Mokan who is Sontri's friend. The political and social parallel of this– managing our affairs equitably– is not as easy as winning political independence. In this context, agitation for political independence is paralleled with the state of courtship. The euphoria of being a new nation, which is equated with the elated state of wining a new love, dies down after a few years of self-rule (marriage) during which the economic lot of the common man is not improved. Femi Fatoba in his thesis quotes one Chief Bagunbe, on Ifa in the verse of Iwori otura, Keke, as saying that: "the name of the male character, is the Yoruba "spindle" while Olomijo stands for "cotton". The spindle is a phallic object while the cotton, soft and cushioning, represents the female"[5] (105). The spinning process, which is a form of dance, is the method by which the cotton changes into thread as it winds round the spindle. Thus Sontri's request to Yajin to "dance with me", assumes a stronger sexual dimension than it seems. It is at this point of dance that Yajin becomes, in spirit, the Olomijo in Iwori otura. The dance is highly symbolic because it is the unifying essence as the request "dance with me" means that both characters have to obey one rhythm, act as one unit, and think a common thought, the dance is of a creative relevance in that it is sexual and therefore a prelude to the arrival of an offspring. On the political ground, it is also creative because the "offspring" could be a new social order both of unity (dance) of new era.

An important note is Osofisan's socialist ideological view point which affects the structure of this play through the introduction of the crawling thing when Yajin sees a common and harmless lizard. The sight of the lizard becomes the excuse to introduce the song about crawling things, which is symbolic of the masses who have no voice in the running of their lives.

> He has no bite he has no fist
> he has no tongue to voice protest
> This millipede, a curious thing
> …It signifies our nation now,
> On shaky feet we stumble on
> We change our skins like chameleon
> Prostrate and mute like crawling
> Things…. (14- 15)

However, Sontri's confrontation with Yajin shows Osofisan's anger with the general complacency of the people he thinks should care about their society. Sontri tells Yajin:

> Those two soft eyes, soft…
> And blind. And those painted eyelids,
> Those gentle curtains nicely cordoned
> Around your sweet romantic dreams, while
> The world groans around you on wounded
> Wings. Close your windows with curfews
> Of indifference….(16)

It is obvious that there are several contexts that have influenced the writing of the play. In *Look Back in Anger*, Jimmy rages against his society at the slightest provocation; so does Sontri in *The Chattering and the Song*. Both characters have the propensity to twist other people's words to suit their purposes. Both show the proverbial artistic temperament and talents, at least, in the writing of songs. And their songs show causative view of their different societies. The only difference is that Jimmy's lyrics are recited while Sontri sings his to the accompaniment of a drum. According to Femi Fatoba's analysis, the similarities extend, and to quote him, "the similarities between the two plays extend even into the particular, such as the use of the word "virgin" as a symbol of innocence – and purity contaminated through inordinate social protection by the members of the "wrong" social class" (137). Jimmy in *Look Back in Anger* says: "Anyone who's never watched somebody dies is suffering from a pretty base case of virginity" (57). Later he tells Helena: "Now leave me alone and GET OUT, You evil-minded little virgin" (73).

Femi Osofisan's Sontri is angry with Funlola after the latter confesses to having driven away the weaverbirds:

> Sontri: You did what!
> Funlola: (Frightened by his savagery) I...I thought they were causing too much commotion...
> Sontri: Commotion! (He is almost hoarse anger)
> Who is this.... this virgin? (17)

Later, in addressing Yajin, he refers to Funlola.

> Sontri: Ignorance! Ignorance again!

No wonder you are good friends!
You'll both end well. Tell me
Suppose I take your pretty virgin
Here before your father, what do
You think will be the verdict? Ehn? (18)

The word "virgin" here connotes purity but its use by the two characters, in the quotation above, shows a tone of derision. Jimmy says "a base case of virginity" which sounds like an attack of a disease. It also suggests that social "copulation" enriches one's experience in dealing with humanity rather than the holier-than-thou or morally stand-offish attitude which sexual chastity connotes. In this context, sexual chastity is equated to moral snobbishness which, according to the working class, is a vice of the middle class.

The word "virgin" as used by Sontri evokes the same image of purity, which was tarnished by ignorance. He could have used any of the words, "fool, dolt, simpleton", which would have created the same impression and made us cultivate that opinion of Funlola. "Virgin" is chosen to show that both characters (Helen and Funlola) in both plays have been protected from experiences which would have enriched or strengthened them socially.

Fatoba argues that the word "virginity" suggests sexual chastity and its use by Osofisan has perhaps been influenced by Osborne. The use of the word "virgin" by the two characters quoted above is derisive and contemptuous. Its use belongs to the "absurd school of dramatists" (140).

The plays explicitly hinge on socio-political and economic freedom, on revolutionary action and for this reason, sees corruption principally from a class structure perspective. It is therefore adequate to assert that: (the play essentially) dramatizes the "process of revolution, and the instrument of revolution...and the underground process of rebellion against the corrupt power-elite" (Obafemi 238). While the play focuses on the problem of exploitation and intimidation in a capitalist state like Nigeria, the flashback situates the action in the feudalist oligarchy of Abiodun, the then Alafin of Oyo. Latoye, organizes the Alafin's guards by exposing the high-handedness and corrupt rule of the oligarchy and succeeds in transforming them into a revolutionary tool to destroy the Alafin. He puts it bluntly to the Alafin just before the final onslaught:

> Yes, you will kill me. But your hands
> Cannot reach the seeds I have already
> Sown, and they are on fertile soil.
> Soon, sooner than you think, they will
> Burst into flower and their scent alone
> Will choke you. (37)

It is believed that, Alafin Abiodun and Basorun Gaha both belong in the same class, hence the change in rulership of one for the other was not an improvement in the social conditions of the people they ruled. In the history of Oyo, Alafin Abiodun overthrew Gaha and replaced military oppression with monarchical tyranny, while in recent Nigerian political history, General Gowon replaced political oppression with military subjugation. It is this political context that provokes the creative sensibility of Osofisan to write this play. Hence he explains:

> [with chattering] I was writing about Gowon. He was in the same situation [as Abiodun]. He'd fought a war, he'd established peace, but the regime had

68

become very corrupt. Also I wrote this play because people seemed to have come to the point of view you could do nothing to displace such a regime (qtd. in Dunton 73).

Therefore, within the socio-political context of *The Chattering and the Song*, Gowon is to Balewa what Alafin Abiodun was to Gaha. Osofian rewrites the history of Oyo during the chaotic period of the rebellious Bashorun Gaha who overthrew the reigning Alafin and set up a reign of terror, killing all the princes of Oyo except Abiodun who was crippled in one leg. Abiodun grew up to challenge and overthrow this despot, re-establishing law and order. By this, it is reasonable to argue that *The Chattering and the Song* passes subtle comment on the post-civil war years of Gowon's military dictatorship. Here Osofisan draws from a historical precedent in pre-colonial Nigeria as a parallel of the present one (although Osofisan wrote against Gowon's regime, it is still relevant to the military regimes of Babangida and Abacha in their reign of terror and corruption), and he shows how tyrannical regimes could be overthrown. Thus Osofisan has fictionalized the facts of history to anticipate a mass revolution. And in the words of Gbilekaa, "Osofisan in a fictive and yet mythopoetic sense, has squeezed the facts of history casting them in an unchronological manner to demonstrate the plasticity of oral tradition" (272). In this way, he recast this historical precedent in the old to suit the demand of contemporary social reality. However, it is important to note that writers like Osofisan should tread with caution on what type of images of our leaders are created by this deliberate distortion of historical facts and figures to gratify their ideological proclivity.

There is incongruity between the new political / military leaders (Gowon, Babangida, Abacha and the likes) who are obviously inhuman, totalitarian and egomaniacs, as opposed to the image of the traditional leader like Alafin Abiodun who is believed from historical fact to be sympathetic, sacrosanct and sacred. Another Nigerian playwright who has shown his disgust with political developments and leadership in Nigeria since independence is Ola Rotimi. In his play *Hopes of the Living Dead*, he has chosen his portion among the masses and the oppressed class by condemning the ideology of the ruling elite. Gbilekaa contends that Rotimi in his recent play "has joined the ranks of Obafemi, Osofisan and Bode Sowande to mirror the changing Nigerian society and to voice the discontent of the exploited class and to herald the dawn of a new era" (9). Rotimi uses historical material in Hopes to avail his audience with the knowledge of the past for the reconstruction or social re-engineering of the present and the future. This enables his audience to put the progress of their society into proper perspective. But in dramatizing history, Rotimi re-orders historical events not only to suit technical and artistic exigencies but also to project certain ideological perceptions. This is clearly reflected in the profile of the production notes:

> Born in Abonnema (Nigeria), in 1905, of Kalabari parentage, IKOLI HARCOURT WHYTE lost his father...and found himself stricken with leprosy about the same time... (The government neglected the leprosy patients) and ... it is at this point that the lepers felt the time had come to impress their modest right to existence upon the complacence of the world conscience. (iv)

In *Hopes*, Rotimi has evoked the historical events surrounding Ikoli Harcort Whyte and his fellow lepers to reflect the collision of men and forces based on socio-historical context. It is another work with political relevance, illustrating that the rights and demands of the masses cannot be stifled by any physical disability. In the play, the lepers revolt against the authority of the oppressive class in their society. They demand a better rehabilitation center and despite their glaring disability, they learn to work in harmony and help themselves. *Hopes of the Living Dead* subtitled "a play of struggle" is based on events in the colonial Nigeria of 1924. In that particular year, Ikoli Harcourt Whyte and forty other lepers were kept in Port-Harcourt General Hospital for an experiment on a cure for leprosy. However, the authorities kicked against such an experiment in a regular hospital. Consequently, Dr. Ferguson eventually had to abandon the research, and leave for his home in Scotland. The leprosy patients were therefore left in a state of hopelessness and helplessness. At this juncture, the patients began to look within for a solution to this nascent problem. The feeling of hopelessness and desperation they experienced in the event of Dr. Ferguson's departure was conveyed by Ikoli to his fellow inmates in the following words:

> From now on, we are alone...
> We fool ourselves if we believe that
> The big men of this place will care for
> Us as before. We fool ourselves if we
> Think the world outside will give us peace
> To continue to be one blood, together,
> In this place children of our fathers

Our struggle has begun. (17)

The climax of the play is the attempt by the hospital authorities, aided by police-agents of the colonial administration, to eject the lepers forcefully from the leprosy wards. The superintendent who is a symbol of colonial authority gives the patients a twenty-four hours ultimatum within which they are to move out of the hospital premises and from the periphery of Port-Harcourt city. This intimidatory posture of the repressive colonial authority and the emerging Nigerian petit-bourgeois will not, however, silence the lepers from asserting at least their right to live and have their being in the society they belong. It is pertinent to reiterate the fact that in *Hopes*, the conflict is not between individuals and their personal desire but between social forces and ideologies. In this allegory, the Nigerian Government is presented here as being despotic, terrorizing the poor, suffering masses, the downtrodden and rural peasants of the Nigerian society whose desperation is likened to the deadly leprosy disease. Rotimi has unarguably used leprosy and the lepers' revolt of 1924 as a metaphor to show that the lepers' struggle against the colonial administration was aimed at discovering and asserting their humanity. *Hopes* thus presents a dialectical analysis of the lepers' revolt in our colonial past and holds the past as a parallel to contemporary Nigerian struggle for a truly democratic society.

In *Hopes*, Rotimi seems to be saying that the person we need to lead us out of "Egypt" our present political quagmire to the promised land of political stability is perhaps a resilient, resourceful, committed, purposeful and visionary leader like Ikoli Harcourt Whyte of the play and not the tribalised, visionless, purposeless, selfish, and greedy leaders we have presently at the seat of power. As a social commentary, Hopes anatomises Nigeria's socio-political image and indeed the so-called Third World's economic dependence, and the impasse of neo-colonialism and further shows how these problems can be overcome by the spirit of communalism and collective efforts of the masses.

Osofisan's *The Chattering and the Song* and Rotimi's *Hopes of the Living Dead* harp on the revolutionary potential of the masses in bringing about a welfarist society. The plays of both first generation playwrights like Ogunde, Soyinka, Clark, Rotimi and Sofola and that of second generation playwrights like Osofisan, Sowande, are critique images of the socio-political and cultural events in their environment.

# Chapter Four

## *A Handcuff to History*

A.Kehinde

AFRICAN writers have the propensity for relating the subject matter of their works to significant events that have taken place in their societies. One of such events is the Mau-Mau uprising in Kenya. Many of the contemporary Kenyan novelists have looked to the Mau-Mau Emergency for their subject matters. In fact, the treatment of this highly volatile and unfortunate political event reveals the links between cultural production and its ideological determinants in African literature. However, while attention has most often been focussed on Ngugi wa Thiong'o because of his fine handling of the Mau-Mau onslaught in his novels, critics tend not to adequately examine the representation of this veritable historical episode in the fiction of Meja Mwangi, another fine writer from Kenya. In this chapter we examine the reconstruction of the Mau-Mau uprising in Mwangi's *Carcase for Hounds* noting that in the novel, Mwangi excels in presenting many different, if often unrecognised, materials on the uprising to the readers of

African literature. It posits that Mwangi's novel has participated in passionate debates about racism and futility of war in human societies, even as it also engages in conversation with precursor texts on Mau-Mau insurgence in Kenya written by some Kenyan colonial settlers and their sympathizers. Mwangi has thus secured a reputation as one of the African writers who have dealt successfully with anti-colonial temper.

Kenya used to be a centre of attraction for the tourists and merchant adventurers from Southern Arabia and India partly because of its weather that was auspicious to the traders. However, before it became an independent nation, while the white settlers and Indian immigrants were enjoying the best farmlands and vast tracts of game reserves for their sporting Safaris, the native Kenyans were given low wages, and they were subjected to colour bar (Gray 126). Their freedoms of speech, movement and the press were severely curtailed. They also had no representatives in the councils of the administration. In spite of bearing the heaviest share of the tax burden, the educational opportunities of the native Kenyans were drastically limited (Chinweizu 69). This confirms the claim that control of political power and struggle over economic resources are two key factors responsible for conflicts and wars in Africa (Oyeshile 2; Alao 190). In 1951, moderate demands for African representation in Kenya's legislative council were turned down. Consequently, African bitterness against the colonialists naturally mounted. Volunteers were made to swear a solemn oath, giving out their lives as sacrifice:

> That if I am called on to kill for our soil,
> If I am called on to shed my blood for it,
> I shall obey and I shall never

surrender (Karuiki 56)

Predictably, the hitherto subtle anti-colonial temper boiled over into the Mau-Mau revolt. In October 1952, a state of Emergency was proclaimed. British troops were airlifted to brutally suppress the revolt. Thus, racial dissonance ensued between the white settlers and the native Kenyans. Segun Adekoya gives an apt reason why revolutions occur in a politically and economically hostile society like Kenya. In his words: "The love solution offered by the great religions of the world emasculates the will and is either completely forgotten or repudiated by nations as they fight for survival" (285). Actually, the causes of the Mau-Mau struggle for independence were numerous and many-sided. That the struggle was embarked upon by the Kenyan people for their political independence is an obvious fact. However, economic and social factors were as prominent causes as the need for political rights. It may not be an over-statement to say that the most prominent causes of the uprising were economic factors, especially the desire to recover the people's stolen lands. Kenyan people believed that the White man had robbed them of their land and were embittered over this because to them land was a symbol of authority, of belonging to a clan, of wealth and continued association with the ancestors who guarantee their continued protection. Ngugi provides a vivid portrayal of the anti-colonial temper in Kenya thus:

> The masses are restive. The nationalist leaders, usually from the ranks of the educated few, organize the discontent into a weapon aimed at the throat of the master. 'Go unto Pharaoh and say to him, Let my people go.' Often the nationalist elite demands

independence in terms of the very Western ideals it was taught at school and in colonial universities. (56)

In fictional and non-fictional narratives, the unique peasant revolt in Kenya tagged Mau-Mau uprising has been reinvented by ideologues on both the Left and Right in postcolonial Africa. This confirms Abiodun Adediran's view which goes thus:

> To convey impressions of the past, poets, playwrights and novelists have long used faction the blend of facts and imagination. In different African countries today, several literary writers, through imaginative reconstructions of the past, vividly bring out the ideas that historians aspire to express. (21)

Also, the accounts given of the event of Mau-Mau uprising point to a situation in which journalists, creative writers and academics alike seem at a loss to interpret what is happening. Optimism is followed by despair; explanations are offered only to be discarded or retracted (Chabad 39). African writers have the propensity for relating the thematic preoccupations of their works to significant events that have taken place in their societies. Afam Ebeogu isolates two of such events that are predominantly captured in African literature –slave trade and the colonial experience. In his words:

> There has been a tendency…to relate the history of written African literature to significant events that have taken place on the continent. According to them, after the slave trade, the major historical event

that gave birth to serious poetry in Africa was the colonial experience. (35)

The production of a mounting body of writings on the historical event of the Mau-Mau uprising suggests an awareness and recognition of its importance in the historical development of Kenya in the works of some of the continent's major writers. However, while due attention has most often been focussed on Ngugi wa Thiong'o because of his fine handling of the event of Mau-Mau (See *The River Between*, *Weep Not, Child*, *A Grain of Wheat* and *Petals of Blood*), critics have generally not adequately examined the presence of this veritable historical episode in the fiction of Meja Mwangi, another major writer from Kenya. To some extent, Mwangi's fiction has attracted considerable interest and attention, but one novel, *Carcase for Hounds*, has always been passed over in critical neglect. A brief look at the novel reveals why an assessment of Mwangi's discourse on Mau-Mau might be necessary. Actually, he has excelled in presenting many different (if often unrecognised) materials on the Mau Mau war to readers of African literature. It can be argued that perhaps one reason for the relative lack of critical appreciation of Mwangi's alternative fictional reconstruction of the war is the ideological difference of the text. The varied nature of his historical re-enactment of the Mau Mau war makes it as enigmatic as it is rewarding (Clarke 171). His handling of the conflict not only provides his own version of that incident already present in some other literary texts but also adds a new dimension to it. Mwangi gives the reader of African historical fiction a text of necessity; he seeks to counter the misrepresentation of Kenya's history by the writers who yielded to the temptation of assuming the disagreeable outlook on the nation's history.

Mwangi's *Carcase for Hounds* reveals that the seeds of racism, ethnicity, disharmony, mediocrity and corporate distrust have been sown in African societies; violence has replaced the hitherto peaceful existence. This validates Ahmad Aijaz's view that "all third-world texts are necessarily national allegories" (101) and Idaevbor Bello's assertion that "the relationship between literature and society is anchored on the fact that the events in the society give being to literature" (101). The tropes of dissonance and pain in the prose text thus become a metaphor for the history of the dislocated, the exiled, the alienated and the stranded, the depressed and deprived African who has been dispossessed of his inheritance and integrity. In fact, resonating through most of Mwangi's novels is the echo of the painful existence of man. Whether this is explicitly stated as in *Carcase for Hounds* and *Kill Me Quick*, or implied by the persistent occurrence of painful situations, as in *Going Down River Road*, or through images and symbols as in *Striving for the Wind*, pain and dissonance constitute a recurring motif in Mwangi's novels which create a motley array of failure and ridiculous figures. The uniqueness of Mwangi's novel about the Mau-Mau war is not only in the thematic focus of the text. What is unique in the text is the style of telling the story with a freshness that makes it different and remarkable. In fact, what makes him stand somewhat above his contemporaries in the imaginative depiction of anti-colonial struggle in Kenya is the way he has used a material that is common to them all.

A pertinent question is worth asking at this stage to illuminate the subject matter of Mwangi's Carcase for Hounds. What powerful forces do the whites constitute in the referent society of the novel? They are unconquerable, and every generation of blacks feels their uncomfortable presence. It is in this almost inhuman climate that General Haraka, the hero of *Carcase for Hounds*, finds himself. As he lives on, his hatred and detestation for the white man's presence for their ill treatment, betrayal and manipulation of his people equally increase. Like a lone voice crying in the wilderness, so psychologically and physically devastated by the whites, the hero rises courageously against the wickedness of the whites and near-slavery conditions of his people. He has too great a heart, too iron-like a determination and far-reaching a vision to be ruffled.

*Carcase for Hounds* begins by an examination of the perennial pain and dissonance in African society. Actually, the first chapter of the novel introduces the reader to the turmoil of racial conflict and also defines the basic attitudes of nearly all the main protagonists. Painful and dissonant scenes dot the novel, and a price is put on Haraka's head. Caught between the two warring races are the frightened and physiologically disturbed villagers of Pinewood and Acacia Ranch. The forest fighters suffer from a lot of astoundingly complex problems. Their lives are made painful by lack of the basic necessities of life. Security or safety needs are totally absent in the society fictionalized in the story. The characters live in a perpetual state of fear. Both camps (Haraka's and Kingsley's) are filled with the aura of fear and insecurity. It is a community where man is hunted like an animal. Cases of death are reported with indifference, without passion,

> The story when it was unfolded turned out to have no complication at all. The home guards had just heard shots from the village. When they went out to

investigate they came across the body. The murderers were gone. Simple as that. It was a straightforward Mau Mau killing. A Haraka thing. (33)

Again, people are wounded and crippled. The whole society witnesses unceasing hardship and a breakdown of mutual understanding and law and order. The story is indeed full of inter-group and intra-group conflicts. As a novel about war, the overall tone of the text is that of gloom and disillusionment. The plot of the story reveals a tension between what Kingsley and Haraka think is happening and what the reader knows is happening. This is a conflict between fact and supposition. Indices of frustration and anguish are vividly evoked to present the hostility of nature elements and society as they reveal the imminence of ultimate failure and death. Specifically, the setting of the novel is used as a thematic vehicle, an index of death, destitution, decay, hollowness and brokenness. Also, the use of complex locales and the handling of the multi-locales in the text are artistically explicit. In the main, the setting of the novel signifies terrible powers, darkness, mystery, terror and discomfort. It possesses a dual nature, with beauty and terror. Besides, it is emblematic of the gloomy nature of the whole struggle between the Mau-Mau warriors and the imperialists.

The physical setting, the level at which the struggle is conducted, encompasses dense forests which are largely impenetrable. The colonial forces, flying in helicopters, are unable to come down because of the thickness of the forests. The entire atmosphere is powerful and gripping. The use of weather in the novel is also symbolic. The repeatedly evoked cloud, storm and rain certainly signify a society in pains and excruciating conflicts. The natural phenomena are metaphors for the unpredictability of history and forces beyond human control. Rain, in a refreshingly African connotation, symbolizes hope and fertility, but in *Carcase for Hounds* it signifies a grim and fatalistic determinism.

Edward Said has offered an illuminating explanation of the import of 'history' in postcolonial writings. He declares:

> Appeal to the past is among the commonest strategies in interpretations of the present. What animates such appeals is not only disagreement about what happened in the past and what the past was, but uncertainty about whether the past really is past, over and concluded or whether it continues, albeit in different forms, perhaps. (33)

Therefore, the hallmark of Mwangi's *Carcase for Hounds* is its historical strain. He exposes and interrogates the factors responsible for conflicts in human societies. However, in this novel, Mwangi, an objective analyst of the distant and contemporary conflicts in Kenya, avoids the tendency of critics who always put all the blames for the plight of the Africans at the doorsteps of the colonial masters. As an artist who exists in the bosom of his ill society, Mwangi attempts to use the novel as a means of partaking in the task of healing the society of its skewed inter-racial relationship. Although colonialism has left an indelible mark on the socio-political, cultural, educational and spiritual structures of the colonized regions, it will be subjective to blame the colonizers for all the woes of Africans. What about the comprador bourgeoisie, the 'nouveaux riches', the more brutal black stooges? The problems of misgovernance and election malpractices in

Kenya which have led to inter-ethnic dissonance, arson, murder and agonies lend credence to the foregoing claim. According to Said:

> Blaming the Europeans sweepingly for the misfortunes of the present is not much of an alternative. What we need to do is to look at these matters as a network of interdependent histories, that it would be inaccurate and senseless to repress, useful and interesting to understand. (19)

The text leaves nothing behind in painting the dissonance between two races, that is, the struggles of Haraka and his band against a superior force. However, Haraka fights on, as if he senses that the only way out of subjugation is determination, perseverance and outright attack of the white man's subtle manoeuvres and manipulations to keep the black man a perpetual slave. To signify the intricate problems of the warriors in both camps,

Mwangi makes use of convoluted plot structure. There is no singularity of plot since the society being fictionalised lacks order, peace and symmetry. With the bifurcated plot, Mwangi is able to expose the reader to what is happening in the camp of the Mau-Mau warriors, and later switches to the happenings in the camp of the colonial soldiers. As a result, the reader is able to have a clear picture and understanding of the events in the novel. Haraka's persistent struggle to set his people free from white political and economic strangulation is a call to every patriotic African to rise to the challenges of liberating his fatherland from undue interference of strangers. In the struggle for total economic and political emancipation, we should not expect an easy victory. There is a price to pay, and this may involve, as in Haraka's case, suffering, hunger, thirst, imprisonment and possibly death.

Since "the history to be found in fiction is imaginary" (Maughan-Brown 13), in analysing *Carcase for Hounds* therefore we need historical conjunctures to which the fiction relates and within which it was produced. A lot of complexities of socio-economic and cultural-ideological factors are silently at work upon the production of the text. In the words of Terry Eagleton, a historical novel "negotiates an already constructed ideological experience of real history" (70). The conflicts in *Carcase for Hounds* are an allegory of a series of cataclysmic socio-political upheavals that include the violent confrontation of the government forces and the forest fighters. Therefore, it is a telescopic summary of Kenya's history or, at least, of its Mau Mau struggle. In the text, Mwangi is able to present fundamental human conflicts in specifically African terms. The conflicts of classes, nature and man, personalities, tribes and families are juxtaposed with those of colonialists hustling against Kenyans' respectability. The subliminal theme of the novel is Kenyan self-sufficiency in all varieties of human relationship, behaviour, suffering and disharmony. The life portrayed is a fierce life-and-death chase between Haraka and the government forces. This is symptomatic of fear and hatred.

The novel also foregrounds the economic exploitation of Kenyan peasants symbolized by the plight of the villagers at Pinewood forest station. The villagers work for the white man, Mr. Jackson, a symbol of the European establishment, who has lured the natives into his service with the promise of farmland, money and western education for their children. However, the people are frustrated at last. They are unsuspectingly dragged into servitude. Thus, the interaction between the Kenyan people and the colonizers, as portrayed in this text, is a kind of master-servant relationship. The peasants, as portrayed in the novel, have been reduced to the background of the economic system. They have thus relinquished their former economic activities for the white men's farms or homes as 'cheap labourers' or 'house boys'.

On the interpersonal level, the dissonance in the novel has an atom of vengeance or personality clashes. Captain Kingsley, a former District Commissioner, who becomes a rival and an enemy to Haraka, a one-time District Chief under him, has some personal scores to settle with him (Haraka) beyond his mission to subdue the Mau-Mau revolt. In fact, the conflict in the novel is personalized by setting up an individual Mau-Mau leader against an opposing colonial military commander. Likewise, Haraka wants Chief Simba's head at all costs; to him, the Chief is a stooge and a traitor. Therefore, the major characters in the novel (Kingsley, Chief Simba and Haraka) become arch-enemies hunting one another with all vigour.

The colonial government is depicted as oppressive, pursuing the forest fighters and their supporters for total elimination. The fighters are subdued and subjected to a life of insecurity. Huts are burnt; men and women are murdered during raids. For instance, Timau Police Post and Pinewood Forest Station are brutally ransacked and burnt down by the forest fighters. There is the problem of scarcity of food that the fighters have to contend with, especially when they are on the move. The bands that Kimamo leads to attack Ol Pejeta are without food for three days in the rain-soaked jungle. The harsh conditions, although slightly different, are not peculiar to the forest fighters. Their colonial opponents also experience similar kinds of natural hostility. They also sleep in cold, sometimes in the rain. Actually, the fighters are always in some kinds of danger. The story is very brutal and arresting –true to both the specific quality of tension that typifies a war-torn society and the more universal psychology of human relationships. The warriors can only keep within the margin of living and death through the supplies coming from loyalists in the village. At times, they have their emissaries shot dead or handed over to the authorities.

The discord between Haraka's band and government forces can be supported with certain ideologies, philosophies and myths of the general strike: Fanon's view of violence as a therapeutic art in the colonial situation, certain forms of Marxism and the Jihad spirit in Islam (62). V.S. Reid in *The Leopard* also endorses the use of violence by liberation movements. The whole story of *Carcase for Hounds* is thus a game of hide-and-seek between opposing interests, a Manichaean dualism in which the black warriors are depicted as carcases.

The story of Haraka's group's agony is counterpointed by the nocturnal activities of these people who deprive themselves of the comfort of their homes and families and must keep on moving from one place to the other, hiding in unusual places at night to conduct their activities. The plight that places this huge burden on their neck is real. They sob so that the weight could be removed; they moan and groan with a view to enjoying the solidarity of their compatriots. In fact, Mwangi uses the fighters as a thematic vehicle to reflect the alienation and individualism most obvious in colonial Kenya.

Unlike the Mau Mau novels of Ngugi, Robert Ruark, Godwin Wachira and the like, *Carcase for Hounds* is a unique Mau Mau novel because it has a different political tone. This difference arises from the fact that, in the novel, racial dissonance is more implicit than explicit, more covert than overt, more deautomatized than foregrounded. The racial dissonance in the novel is much more sublime than the politics we come about in other novels about the Mau Mau. Unlike the more traditional novels about racism, the politics in this novel is subsumed under a framework of egoistic adventures. This ideological stance is perhaps borne out of many factors: consideration of implied readers, objectivity and an attempt at revisionist intertextuality. Thus, Mwangi's interpretation in *Carcase for Hounds* is creative; it does not unartistically and strictly comply with socio-historical realities.

The psychological effects of the Mau-Mau war on villages and districts are also very agonizing. This arises out of social, economic and political subjugation of the black men by the colonial forces. The forest fighters face the psychological torture of estrangement, hostility and family disintegration. Actually, the tone of the novel is pervading, polemical and elegiac. The search for meaning out of darkness and tension in the society has incited a precipitous tone in the text. The reader is confronted with the tone and mood of doom and gloom. This is portrayed on two planes —on individual nation-state (nation waging war against nation), and on individual relationships as shown in the conflicting relationships between Haraka and Simba. Chris Wanjala supports this view:

> The real mark of sacrifice in the Kenyan's freedom was in his capacity to estrange himself from his family in order to concentrate his genius to the liberation of his people... those who fight for the

cause have to give up all they have and are to hostile world of the forest, in search for freedom. (34)

Haraka's choice of rebellion puts him outside the mainstream of society, but he continues to do battle with the forces of convention in order to find the spiritual truths that will preserve social vitality. Worse still, it is commonplace within the context of African political system and administrative setting to misconstrue freedom-fighting activities as an act of rebellion and youthful exuberance. The imbroglio between the colonial and anti-colonial forces also represents a snowball of dialectic relations between the state and the agents of revolution. The trends in inter-racial dissonance are complicated by the fact that even, among themselves, the blacks mostly resolve their conflicts by the same method of violence. For instance, the peasants in *Carcase for Hounds* are highly critical of the home guards and the security forces. Unfortunately, the colonial forces take advantage of the cracks in the solidarity of the people.

Nature is also depicted in the text as possessing a dual characteristic. It is at times genial and benign to the two warring groups; at times it is cruel. Initially, the pendulum of its favour swings towards the forest fighters, but unfortunately, in the end, it turns against them. Due to the inhibiting factor of the weather, rain, rivers and storm, Haraka and his group are trapped in a cave. The picture we have of them is that of vagabonds and destitutes. They become archetypal wild men, with strange demonic potency. They look quasi-bestial with their red eyes and are depicted as shaggy and unkempt in their tattered clothes.

The forest area, Laikipia District, which is the hideout of the freedom fighters, also constitutes an impediment to the achievement of the goals of both groups. It does not allow the government's force to pursue the forest fighters into the jungle, and it encourages poor visibility from cold, morning wind, humid warmth and wet undergrowth that are all indices of uncertainty and pains of life. The overflowing Gura River claims the lives of some of the Mau-Mau warriors. For instance, Kimani, a devout supporter of Haraka, is drowned in the river as they are returning from a raid, and the Nanyuki River checks the attempted flight of Kimamo. Rain, which almost assumes the role of a character in its different manifestations in the story, also inhibits the warriors from carrying out their operations. Such is the fate of the people fighting for the total emancipation of their nation.

In pain, Haraka sees his hope dashed and can do nothing to save it after all his efforts had failed. After his active days, he becomes helpless, incompetent and indecisive. At this stage, his tentacular force is being greatly undermined by combined forces of man and nature. The reader now encounters an image of a helpless and trapped animal. In the cave, where he and his group hibernate, he is fed like a dog or an infant. The pervading atmosphere is that of despair, hunger, madness and hopelessness. He even shoots his putative successor (Kimamo) out of mental tumult and social angst. The end of the novel depicts the once active general as holed up in the cave, fatally wounded, mentally derailed and gradually dying of gangrene. In the text, through the technique of stream of consciousness, the reader is introduced to some of the problems facing the black man in his own land. This is with a view to exposing the dehumanising effects of colonialism in Africa. The reader witnesses the painful end of General Haraka when he reminisces about his goals, their implementation and the consequent failures: "In his mind, General Haraka saw a team of ragged little offspring with running noses playing in the mud outside a cold hut…" (7).

Unfortunately, the hard-worn independence in Kenya, as in many other neo-colonial African countries, does not make the lives of the peasants better. Neocolonialsm, in Kenya, is a form of imperialism through the agency of the new comprador bourgeoisie, the new ruling elite who have dashed the emancipatory promise of nationalist struggle (Chinweizu 72). The heroes of the Mau-Mau revolt are now casualties (Obafemi 21). They are presently the debris of society –men with a brave past but with no future; the hitherto rhetoric of utopianism is now being replaced by that of disillusionment. Thus, the postcolonial novel is replete with indices of anger, fatalism and despair with a view to ascertaining that the neo-colonial leaders have betrayed the revolutions and the masses (Lazarus 41; Roscoe 19). Ngugi, in his much-cited work, *Homecoming*, captures the frustrating effect of the anti-colonial struggle in Kenya:

> Independence has not given them back their land. They are still without food or clothes. But now there is a difference. Before independence basic realities were boldly and visibly delineated: all conflicts were reduced to two polarities – white was wealth, power and privilege; black was poverty, labour and servitude. 'Remove the white man,' cried the nationalist leaders, 'and the root cause of our troubles is gone.' Gone? Not exactly! The peasants and workers are still the hewers and carriers, but this time, for what Aluko would call the 'black White Man'. (56)

Haraka's pain is an epitome of the agony of the black man in the hands of the colonialists. Once an agile man, a superman, a controller and motivator of men, he now becomes dejected and mentally derailed, doing his last battle with death. His gangrenous condition is also exacerbated by the hostile nature. Thus, the pain persists; he becomes helpless, dejected and hopeless. His last days are marred by slow death. This portrays a profound sense of entrapment and asphyxiation resulting from remorse, as he and his followers feel frustrated and hapless about a way of escape.

In the end, we see Haraka ruminating on the state of his mind, as an individual under extreme psychological and physical pressures. He moves from the consideration of racial and social relationship to the verbal plane, the deeper and less rationally accessible level where there is to be seen at work a pervasive influence from mystic or quasi-mystic forces, a system of pulls and currents. Actually, some subterranean spirits, calling to him, are merely aspects of his disturbed psyche. The psychological upheaval is shown in Mwangi's use of narrated monologue, in which we are introduced to the labyrinths of the General's mind. In his subconscious mind is the picture of Chief Kamau with his head falling off. This scene is replete with images of hatred and difficulties. It contributes artistically to the overall tone of the novel that is stuffed with atavism and hardship. This enlists the reader's sympathy for the forest fighters.

Mwangi's pessimistic candour does not escape our notice. In the precinct of the cave where Haraka and his followers are hibernating, a hyena has been crying for the past three days. The persistent wailing of the hyena is an index of the ruthless forces of the colonial government that are closing in on the band. The cackling of the hyena from a nearby tree is a powerful symbol of the futility of human aspiration: "From somewhere near the cave in the dark, the hyena laughed, a sarcastic chuckle that rose and fell bubbling on the sea of dark silence, then gradually wafted into time herself, eternity" (134).

This is an existential black out. The only exit offered Haraka is death, both psychic and physical. With the laughter of the hyena, Mwangi seems to be suggesting that violence is not the right solution to human misery. It seems he is an apostle of suffering in silence. A possible Marxist interpretation of the "fall" of Haraka is that Mwangi's thesis, provided by historical hindsight, seems to be that the victory of the conquering individualized heroes (like Haraka) neither constitutes a genuine advance nor a liberating tonic for even the marginalized and colonized people. By this artistic means, the local feudal class is magically transferred into a heroic underdog, and this probably provides the impetus for the novel. Thus, Haraka is historically doomed as a representative of a perishing class. His camp is depicted as a metaphor for an ugly 'chamber' of feudal oppression.

Uniting all the forms of pains that are presented in *Carcase for Hounds* is the underlying sense of failure that marks the end of the novel. Each of the characters fails to realize his goal. Therefore, lack of self-actualization is a motif in Mwangi's novelistic repertoire (Eko 185). Man is depicted as a born-failure, with little chance of success. This is the overriding statement of the novel. Haraka fails to achieve his objective. Also, Captain Kingsley, a human hound, let loose by the real hounds –Brigadier Thames and his Emergency Council– fails to capture Haraka alive. Hence, the hyena laughs sarcastically as if celebrating the foolishness of men, the futility of their efforts, their doomed existence, and suggestively pushes this failure into eternity.

However, from the perspectives of African metaphysics and postcolonial discourse, that Haraka, a daring and courageous patriot, dies is not the point; every human being must suffer the angst of finitude. Even at death, Haraka is apotheosised and deified. It is expected that his death will give rise to many more pro-freedom fighters. Thus, Haraka strives that his people are pulled out of the abyss of exploitation and dehumanization. As a great figure whose noble vision orchestrates the yearnings of the oppressed blacks, he is revered and fondly called "General". In the novel, Mwangi artistically maintains a true-to-life and realistic portraiture of the warriors. For instance, Haraka sparingly uses words; he believes in actions.

Mwangi in the novel is conciliating in his posture over racial dissonance. He opts for a syncretic view of life that is, the black and the white should blend into a harmonious whole. This latter time anti-violence strain skews towards the Christian doctrine of "turning the other cheek" (Matthew: 5: 39), and Satyagrahar Gandhi's philosophy of non-violent resistance. Actually, Mwangi, in the novel, believes that war is an ill wind that brings nobody any good. On the whole, he is able to record the prices paid by the colonized in the past with a view to reducing the pain of the present. The important point in these horrendous scenarios in the African setting, which is depicted in Mwangi's text, is that dissonance is a ubiquitous phenomenon in human society. Mwangi attempts to conceive of dissonance in its trans-national and ubiquitous perspective. It has become an albatross, a recurring impediment to societal growth. The narrator of the story therefore notes:

According to the Kenyan Broadcasting Corporation, nothing much was new in the world. The MRLF terrorists had derailed a train in North Jarole. The Americans and the Communists were still at stalemate in Cambodia. The White House had accused the Kremlin of fomenting revolutions in Latin America. The Kremlin had in turn ... Hell. (107)

Another important, yet disturbing, feature of the novel is Mwangi's very ambivalent attitude to the Mau Mau uprising. This is evident in his negative descriptions of the warriors: "As the tall, brutish terrorist stood over him..." (36), as well as his references to them as "blasted Mau Mau" (9) and "murderers" (15, 45, 128). Elizabeth Knight sees this as "studied neutrality" (148). Again, the individuation of Haraka's character as a super human being smacks of relegating the rebellion to an egocentric act. The death of Haraka, as revealed in the novel, signifies the end of the struggle. Perhaps, the point being made, here, by Mwangi is that not all are born to lead; some are born as perennial followers. This is shown in Kimamo's hesitation, like the biblical Joshua, when the mantle of leadership falls on him: "He wished the general was hale and sound, leading the band, and he just a following" (124).

Roger Kurtz sees the ideology of Mwangi in his novel of anti-colonial struggle as an effort to revise the history of the revolt in order to downplay the heroism of the guerrilla fighters and emphasize, instead, "the role of Jomo Kenyatta and other post-independence political leaders" (116). Mwangi has therefore joined some biased writers in criminalizing the Mau Mau revolt. The story is sated with race myths and stereotypes which reincarnate the Eurocentric "atavism" and "primitivism" of "darkest Africa". However, despite this seeming ideological flaw, Mwangi has been able to offer a fundamental solution to the problem of racial and ethnic conflicts in Africa in particular and the whole world in general. His credo is that "what is needed in this millennium is the ability of disparate races and ethnic groups to come together to confront the challenges posed by globalization" (Kehinde 54).

Due to the initial failure of the African writers to "tell their own stories" themselves, some foreign writers took the advantage to construct the stories for them. The stories were predictably marred with racial prejudice. This is the assertion of Ernest Emenyonu. In his words: "No one except us can tell our story and when we relinquish this God-given right, foolish foresters stray in and mistake the middle of a mighty African boar for an African tree trunk" (1). Thus, following the lead of Chinua Achebe, Mwangi, like many other East African writers (especially Ngugi), gave a postcolonial riposte to the hitherto jaundiced and lopsided portrayal of the guerrilla war against British imperialism in Kenya (Mau Mau), its objectives and its executors. This claim supports Sarah Anyang Agbor's that:

> Literature, moreover, participates in the process of shaping collective memories and of subversively undermining culturally dominant memories by establishing counter-memories, which seek to counter, for example, gender-conscious or ethnic perspectives on past events. (187)

Although Mwangi's ideology in the text is flawed, it is still a modest attempt to put the record straight on the Mau-

Mau insurrection in Kenya. His text has therefore participated in passionate debates about racism and the futility of war in human societies, even as it also engages in conversation with precursor texts on Mau-Mau insurgence written by some Kenyan colonial settlers and their sympathizers like Robert Ruark, Elspeth Huxley, Charles Mangua and G.R Fazakerley.

Consequently, the story is both counter-hegemonic and pro-hegemonic. It is counter-hegemonic because it is a critique of what the members of the ruling class (the white land usurpers) have taken for granted. It is, in that wise, a tale of instability and alterability, accepting the need for change. However, it is pro-hegemonic because it is partly iterative; it emphasizes some popular Eurocentric notions about the Mau-Mau war. From this conjunction of hegemonic and counter-hegemonic strains is born a realistic fiction that is not apishly anti-establishment or foolishly pro-establishment. Perhaps, the failure of the guerrilla warriors to achieve their objectives shows colonialism to be an unconquerable, oppressive, expropriation and exploitative process (Aijaz 72). In fact, with Carcase for Hounds, Mwangi secures a reputation as one African writer to deal successfully with the anti-colonial temper. He has used the text to evaluate the past as well as the present, and the nature of inter-ethnic/racial relations in Africa. His sensitive imagination has provided a fresh perspective in the discourse of Kenya's history.

# Chapter Five

## *Voices: Crying in the Desert*

J.Corrado

THE emergence of Angolan literature is traditionally associated with the publication of *Espontaneidades da Minha Alma* (1849) [My soul's outpourings], a collection of poems written by José da Silva Maia Ferreira. Strongly influenced by Brazilian Romanticism and particularly by Gonçalves Dias' native pride, José da Silva Maia Ferreira (1827-1867) celebrated his homeland through a mixture of local topics on one side and typical European romantic forms on the other, revealing aspects of the social life shared by the Luso-African bourgeoisie based in Luanda and Benguela. A second phase, developed during the 1880s and 1890s by Alfredo Troni (1845-1904), Pedro Félix Machado (c. 1860), and Joaquim Dias Cordeiro da Matta (1857-1894), is rather marked by Portuguese Realism, and its distinction resides in the fact that, in the texts produced at this stage, natives are frequently depicted as individuals to whom social ascension is not totally precluded within an intermediate space existing between the discursive space of African textual traditions and the personal relations with

Portuguese masters. Then, with the advent of the new century, Angolan literature entered a phase that can be defined as fully nativist, marked by the claim to equality, fraternity and by a conscious and peremptory attitude inclined toward autonomist pretensions. The members of the so-called 'Generation of 1900' to whom this article is dedicated, Pedro da Paixão Franco (1869-1911), António Joaquim de Miranda (1864-?) and, later, António de Assis Júnior (1887-1960) inherited the legacy of their predecessors and developed different forms of civic struggle.

Paradoxically, the settling-down of Portugal's first Republic (1910), so long desired by many members of the Luanda intelligentsia, managed to definitively wipe out both the Portuguese monarchy and the relative freedom of expression allowed to overseas territories during previous administrations. When it was clear that the depreciation of their status of African-born residents exposed them to blatant discrimination, the native sons of the land hoped to restore their privileges and regain access to social functions once largely performed by their ancestors by focusing their efforts on a campaign program aimed at pleading for easier access to higher education. This solution, however, proved to be quite ineffective: if a purblind Enlightenment belief in education probably did not facilitate the comprehension of the Portuguese colonial project, thereby distorting the meaning of their political struggle, the failure of such proposals can also be attributed to adaptation or intimidation induced by increasing repression. De facto, during the first years of the republican regime, the colonial apparatus was greatly reinforced by the introduction of measures until then practically non-existent in Angola: operational military deployment utilized to secure the conquest of the territory and crush internal resistance; police and administrative repression, detention, deportation, arbitrary suspension and dismissal of native functionaries; complicity or collaboration of some more vulnerable elements of the local elite.

Moreover, it has to be said that the basis of the Portuguese educational heritage was aristocratic and the masses had extremely limited access to education. The keystone of this system was the parish priest and the parochial school. Translated to Africa, this meant that before there could be a school, there would have to be a parish. For there to be a parish, there would have to be an administrative post. As a provision of government service, education was dependent upon administrative expansion: only when the problem of penetration and conquest was solved could the local administration show increased concern for the expansion of public schools (Samuels 124). Individual attempts by governors to assert a provincial educational policy and strengthen school organization failed due to the reluctance of the authorities in Lisbon, the lack of budgetary freedom, insufficient funds, inadequate supplies, etc. If during the last three decades of the nineteenth century access to positions of importance in the government was available to those with ambition and some educational attainment, this informal route to success gradually closed. By 1914, hard work and ability meant nothing without the formal piece of paper attesting to five years of secondary school.

In this way, the conscious refusal of the metropolis to provide education effectively limited the opportunities for equality in Angola. That is the main reason why the 1900s and 1910s saw a mounting wave of protest mainly focused on the nineteenth-century ideal of education. In Luanda the protest assumed more radical forms and, for a brief period, the local militant press was supported by public demonstrations and marches. Such events were led and organized by António Joaquim de Miranda.

## António Joaquim de Miranda

António Joaquim de Miranda (1864-?) engaged a fierce - albeit fruitless- struggle for the education of both 'civilized' and 'non-civilized' natives. Mário António de Oliveira Fernandes, Angolan scholar and poet, recorded the poor success of his initiatives:

> In a normal act, hundreds of association members marched through the streets of Luanda and presented their statutes to the Governor-General. The Governor warmly received both the marchers and their requests, but statutes were never passed, and there was no government action on any of the items requested. (A Formação 134)

Yet Miranda, a civil servant and journalist who considered himself African as much as Portuguese, kept on trying to change the system from within. Between 1908 and 1915, his campaign for education demanded a deep reform of society, to be realized through the formation of citizens in primary, secondary and professional schools. Expounded in a number of articles in both local and metropolitan periodicals, Miranda's project was essentially based on the presumption that civilization and social change are closely dependent on the degree of education attained by citizens. In his own words, "the lack of education amongst the masses not only has the convenience of disaggregating social classes and preventing them from any collective action but, as a result of the lack of solidarity towards a common objective, it also makes progress impossible" (Miranda 1).

In this way Miranda denounced colonial obscurantism, its political meaning and its ill-fated consequences for the colony and its inhabitants. Miranda demanded, together with the implementation of the republic in Portugal and the autonomy of Angola, better educational opportunities for the natives. To this purpose he also founded the volunteer association Educação do Povo-Assistência Mútua [Peoples Education-Mutual Assistance]. Miranda's program, however, moved beyond such relatively harmless forms of protest or association and got closer to a direct claim of independence when he started to invite the totality of his fellow countrymen to boycott tax payment. As the consolidation of the colonial project in Angola increased the fiscal burden on the natives, Miranda's campaigns were aimed at boycotting the payment of compulsory taxes such as the imposto indígena [native tax] -or 'personal annual tax'- and the imposto de cubata [shack tax]. As a consequence of this new campaign, he had to share the common fate of almost all the native sons of the land who tried to extend to the twentieth century -one of colonial implantation, as far as Angola is concerned- ideas and solutions developed during the nineteenth century. After being removed from his administrative duties, Miranda was transferred to Malange, in Northern Angola. There, he resumed his civil activities under close observation of the colonial authorities, as shown in the following article dated 1914. The text, addressed to "all those who are interested in the progress and civilization of Angola, and especially to my fellow countrymen", appeared in a local publication:

Once again I am portrayed as a dreadful revolutionary, capable of promoting a general conflagration aimed at achieving the independence of Angola. I suppose this is the intention that is imputed to me; it appears to be the only one that can possibly corroborate this nonsense of a native revolution in Malange. I hear that they keep tabs on me, because I am considered to be the president of an association of mata-brancos [killers of whites] and the leader of native forces that, one of these nights, would storm white people's houses, and the same happened in Luanda, in October 1911, when I also had to face administrative enquiry because of similar rumours (...) Once again I want to declare that I am not a politician. If 'being political' means struggling for the common good uncompromisingly, then I am political. Concerned with welfare, union, fraternity, progress and civilization, I do not make distinctions based on race or skin colour." (Almeida 646)

Shortly after this, Miranda was definitely deported to Cabinda under the accusation of hindering tax collection.

Pedro da Paixão Franco

Beyond reflecting the constant persecution suffered by the native sons of the land who openly dared to challenge the colonial order, the life and death of Pedro da Paixão Franco can be regarded as a symbol of the destructive rivalries embedded within the Luso-African elite. Son of a black family from Dondo, Pedro da Paixão Franco (1869-1911) was born in Luanda, where he found an employment in the local administration. In 1901 he began an eventful collaboration with Francisco das Necessidades Ribeiro Castelbranco, director of *Almanach - Ensaios Literarios* [Almanac - Literary essays]. *Almanach* featured columns of public usefulness (instructions on fire alerts, formal mourning attire, bank holidays, saints of the day and lunar phases) anecdotes, curiosities, jokes and charades, notes dedicated to local monuments and transcriptions or translations of poems written by renowned authors. But, most of all, readers were invited to submit their articles, tales, verses and riddles. In one of these articles, "O Fanfarrão" [The Braggart], Pedro da Paixão Franco produced a description of the typical young dandy, taking inspiration from Eça de Queirós, who had introduced the figure of the young flâneur in Portugal in works such as *O primo Basilio* [Cousin Basil, 1878] and *A Correspondência de Fradique Mendes* [Correspondence of Fradique Mendes, 1900]. The resentment displayed by the author towards the category of Portuguese residents that, without any doubt, more than any other annoyed the local elite is clear. The depicted character is an elegantly dressed theatre habitué, cynical and overconfident, convinced that he is urbane and loved by women, constantly boasting about his presumed musical talent and bullfighting skills. Always ready to say mean things and making repeated reference to his powerful friends, he is unable to notice that people taunt him and, since he spends much more than he should, that he is constantly beset by creditors (O Fanfarrão 17).

More focused on local actuality, Pedro da Paixão Franco's commemoration of legendary Angolense journalist José de Fontes Pereira (1823-1891) is proceeded by Victor Hugo's quotation 'Quel est son crime? - Le droit'. Paixão Franco then shows his "admiration for the revered patriot who fought all through his glorious life for the benefit of his and my beloved country" (Álas à honestidade 35). Fontes Pereira had died of pneumonia aged 67, and Paixão Franco remembers the titanic war waged by the journalist between 1882 and 1885 when, entrenched in the columns of the republican journal O Pharol do Povo, he censored vice and exalted virtue. The eulogy goes on to praise Fontes Pereira's erudition and simplicity, modesty and liberality, but more striking is the author's leave taking, based on a great sense of pride for his roots and on the refusal of the usual cliché portraying Africans as ignorant, thick-headed and unable to express feelings or emotions in 'civilized forms' such as writing:

> Now do not tell me that I am praising a dead man without knowing what I am actually doing just because I live surrounded by the darkness of ignorance. No! This epitaph, written in loneliness by a rough common man living far away from society, is as sincere as is every thing proceeding from the People, whom I consider my equal. We, the zeros, are not able to use sophistry. (38)

In 1907 Paixão Franco founded the newspaper O Angolense with Francisco Castelbranco, Augusto Silvério Ferreira and Eusébio Velasco Galiano, but their partnership came to an abrupt end when Paixão Franco's colleagues refused to share the responsibility for an article concerning the allegedly unjust discharge of a native functionary. The discharge in question proved to be well motivated and the Governor-General branded the article as defamatory (Dias 88). Paixão Franco wrote a bitter denunciation of the event, *História de uma traição* [History of a betrayal] a publication in two volumes first published in Luanda in 1909. *História de uma traição* is a quite monotonous work, repeatedly emphasizing the author's indignation and the vileness of his former friends' behaviour. Nonetheless, despite its lack of literary value, this text is particularly interesting because it unveils many aspects of Luanda society. First of all, the characters portrayed are all representative personalities of the local intelligentsia: Castelbranco and Paixão Franco were responsible for the only two publications encouraging local literary aspirations at the beginning of the century, *Luz e Crença* and *Almanach - Ensaios Literarios*. Moreover, Paixão Franco's personal experience is extremely important because it allows a better understanding of the nature of the rifts that existed within the Luso-African elite: such divisions would ineluctably lead to the failure of its claims and to its virtual disappearance from twentieth century colonial society.

Paixão Franco also took part in the production of *Voz de Angola clamando no deserto* [The voice of Angola crying in the desert, 1901], probably the most important manifestation of protest against colonial rule ever expressed by the Luanda Luso-African elite. In História de uma traição Paixão Franco explained how a commission was formed, how the members collected the money and printed a thousand copies of *Voz de Angola*, how they decided that the collection of selected articles had to remain anonymous. Francisco Castelbranco and Silvério Ferreira, members of the same commission, successfully submitted their articles. Paixão Franco, instead, contributed financially but saw his article rejected because he had refused to erase his signature from it (*Perspectiva* 253).

António de Assis Júnior

António de Assis Júnior (1887-1960), from Golungo Alto, was a black man to whom the government permitted the practice of law even without being licensed. He worked as a district solicitor and advised the native population about matters mostly concerning land expropriation, earning the reputation of "the natives' lawyer". As a journalist and writer, he took an active role in promoting social, economic and political reforms during the 1910s, protesting against the practice of forced work and denouncing the abuses committed by colonial administrators. In 1917 he was arrested in Dala Tando and detained in Luanda under the accusation of leading a nativist movement whose purpose was to spread rebellion in the colony. No matter how well grounded those accusations were, the immediate reaction of the government against suspects based in both Luanda and its hinterland found the native sons of the land completely unprepared to defend themselves:

> we were imprisoned in the fortress, accused of being involved in a plot of natives against the sovereignty of the Portuguese republic, and the local press, led by men of great intellectual capacity, did not say a single word whether in favor or against that. In the meanwhile prisons filled up with civilized natives proceeding from Golungo Alto, Lucala, Dala Tando, Malange, Novo Redondo, Lubango etc. (Assis Júnior, Relato 2 20)

A few years later, in 1922, an uprising against the colonial regime was mounted in Catete, about forty miles from Luanda. In the aftermath of the Catete revolt, Assis

Júnior was the main defendant in the trial following a series of police investigations, interrogations and arrests occurred in Angola's main urban centres. At that time Assis Júnior was also the director of O Angolense, a newspaper notoriously leading and supporting the cause for the autonomy of Angola. As a consequence of the governmental reaction O Angolense was closed down, together with the African League and the printers Mamã Tita, which had published some of Assis Júnior's work. Furthermore, a good number of intellectuals and journalists were exiled to Cabinda and East Timor. Assis Júnior and other representatives of the intellectual scene shared the fate of about a hundred peasants who had marched from Catete to Luanda to present their claims to High Commissioner Norton de Matos. He spent the last years of his life as a political prisoner in Portugal, where he eventually lectured on Kimbundu at the Superior Colonial School in Lisbon.

The author of a witness statement entitled *Relato dos Acontecimentos de Dala Tando e Lucala* [An account of the events occurred in Dala Tando and Lucala, 1918] and of the novel *O Segredo da Morta, Romance de Costumes Angolenses* [The secret of the Dead, a novel about Angolense customs, 1935], Assis Júnior also left a Kimbundu-Portuguese grammar, further evidence of the influence exerted by Cordeiro da Matta's work on the generation of writers emerging at the beginning of the twentieth century. His best-known work, *O Segredo da Morta*, was published by the newspaper *A Vanguarda* in 1929, appearing as a book only in 1935, when the "voice crying in the desert" had already been silenced. As a matter of fact, this romance appeared in a context dominated by the launch of colonial literature contests and by the consequent profusion of texts serving as vehicles for

Portuguese colonialist propaganda. This is why *O Segredo da Morta* is generally considered as the main literary output of a period often defined as almost 'devoid of literature' even if, according to Portuguese scholar Rita Chaves, it was written about two decades before its appearance as a book (Chaves 42-43).

The romance is set during the 1890s and features some flashbacks to the gilded age of the Luso-African elite, but it also provides a detailed and articulate portrait of that part of the native population that, even having limited or nonexistent access to education, was nonetheless exposed to Portuguese culture and, more or less consciously, contributed to enforcing Portuguese rule. A clear example of that is provided by the following description of native auxiliary troops, the backbone of the Portuguese army during the time of the pacification wars:

> These soldiers, daring and fierce when they had to hunt the enemy down, took the place of the old empacaceiros for they were the first to attack. They offered important services to the national cause, in the conquest and pacification of the inner regions controlled by rebel savages (...) Exception made for the ammunition in wartime, they did not receive any pay or food: as it was for the old auxiliary troops, their main reward consisted of plunder. (*O Segredo* 91)

*O Segredo da Morta*, one of the most precious testimonies of late nineteenth century African society, is set in the area where the Portuguese influence made possible the formation of socio-cultural forms leading to the establishment of a distinct culture. Luanda, together with the region crossed by the Kwanza River, was its centre, while an extensive trade network was its vehicle of diffusion. It is not by chance that, in addition to the two main female characters – the mestizo Elmira and the black Ximinha Cangalanga – a third important character in *O Segredo da Morta* is the river Kwanza, since the flood regime significantly influenced the quotation of agricultural products on the market, interrupted or allowed railway construction, made navigation and penetration inland possible or impossible. Moreover, beyond the economic activities undertaken by the main characters, Assis Júnior did not forget to relate their participation in the two coexisting cultures. The traditional one emerged from the accurate description of funerals, rites and local beliefs, while the creole culture was portrayed, for instance, when Assis Júnior opened the doors of the salon animated by the formidable mulatto mistress of Luanda, Dona Ana Joaquina dos Santos Silva. Elsewhere, the author's attention is also often focused on the special kind of relations linking European and African societies, their relative interpenetration but, most of all, their points of attrition. That is evident in a scene dedicated to the preparation for the celebrations in honour of the 1648 Restoration, an event that was originally intended to "cement a centuries-old fraternization and the harmony between two races":

> Anyway, all that did not prevent two non-native associates from informing the council administrator (...) that the natives, apparently gathered to participate in dances and celebrations, were in fact collecting funds, through the association to which they belonged, in order to set up a rebellion. The truth is that nobody was planning rebellions or

revolts (…) According to what they said, they just wanted to collect some money for the promotion or the appointment of local corporals and sergeants. (O Segredo 148-149)

*O Segredo da Morta* can indeed be considered as a singular work, mainly because of its cultural hybridism. According to literary critic Russell Hamilton, by trying to give life to a cultural duality and, at the same time, preserve the integrity of a series of ambivalences related to the clash between tribal native 'primitivism' and the positivist norms of 'civilization', Assis Júnior produced a real literary alphabet soup "whose lack of organization reflects the ideological confusion of the 'assimilated' intellectual" (Hamilton 56). Hamilton emphasized the fact that Assis Júnior was absolutely sure about his Angolanness and was among the first Angolan intellectuals to foster a political and cultural conscience among black, mixed-race and white fellow countrymen, to formulate a concept of Angolan nationality and to elevate his cultural pretensions to the level of political conflict.

Following a similar line of thought, Portuguese scholar José Luís Pires Laranjeira identified in Assis Júnior's romance the lack of structural clearness and insight which is required of artworks that mark an age, together with the lack of symbolic and paradigmatic significance which could turn it into a national example or into an international reference point. However, especially in many passages of the novel in which the main characters are natives rather than white settlers, the specificity of the social and spatial representation is regarded as a notable achievement. According to Pires Laranjeira this specificity, also originating in the deep influence exerted on the plot line by a traditional religiousness that incorporated some Catholic elements, eventually defined its unequivocal Angolanness (*Laranjeira* 50). Even if lacking the literary and socio-cultural depth that characterised *O Segredo da Morta*, Assis Júnior's account of the events at Dala Tando and Lucala nonetheless deserves some attention, since it deals with a decisive moment for the fate of the Luso-African elite. The text's main purpose is in fact to inform the public about the real causes which led to the wave of arrests of native sons of the land supposedly involved in a nativist movement.

In 1917, after the news broke that frightful atrocities against white settlers had been committed at Seles and Amboim, the white community grew restless and uneasy. The fear of a widespread rebellion led to a certain degree of paranoia and both the press and commercial associations were alerted. Reports stated that 'civilized' natives, supported by rival colonial powers, spread among the 'uncivilized' mass the belief that Portugal was weak and that the government was not able to stifle rebellions. According to the colonial logic, there was no doubt that 'black savages' were totally incapable of outlining, planning and orienting an organized revolt: 'civilized' Africans had necessarily to be the culprits (*Relato* 2 51).

Assis Júnior, who worked as a judicial solicitor in the Golungo Alto district and dealt with both white and black clients, was among the first to be arrested. According to his point of view, the Portuguese practiced hegemony and power politics under the pretext of facing a revolution organized by a troublesome social segment which it was time to substitute with European settlers. From the pages of *Relato dos Acontecimentos de Dala Tando e Lucala* it clearly emerges how the Luso-African society, once so vital in facilitating the implantation of the colonial regime, at this stage had become an obstacle to the control and ultimate domination of Angola. To such an extent that it started to be perceived as a source of danger:

> To us, the revolt of the natives in Angola is already an old, empty and meaningless issue, but to others it is still a powerful avalanche that they can use in order to achieve their purposes - good or bad, we do not know. In this confusion of group interests, self-interest and general greed (...) everything is legitimate and acceptable. Thus, the black man becomes a target and a tool for the conquest of advantages and privileges never obtained before. Any family gathering held at any native's home is immediately considered as a rehearsal for revolution, an attack on the institutions. (*Relato* 1 5)

Assis Júnior's words in defence of the 'black man' can be misleading since, for instance, not even the serious risk of definitive submission and eventual extinction prompted a better understanding and mutual identification between 'civilized' and 'uncivilized' natives. Assis Júnior was a black man who defended and assisted the natives on land ownership matters, but that did not prevent "the natives' lawyer" from displaying prejudices shared by both white settlers and the local elite:

> Three hesitant and shy natives appeared (...) I asked them to come over and advised them to appeal to the authorities whenever they felt threatened, so that they could be defended from any attack. Being individuals of inferior intelligence, I thought best to instill into them respect and trust in authority. (*Relato* 1 10)

Once imprisoned, Assis Júnior was obviously worried about his fate. He feared being treated as a mere 'native' and, unveiling an aspect of Cordeiro da Matta's biography unknown to other sources, remembered the black poet who reportedly suffered similar treatment:

> No news yet, even if I realize that my fate is being decided and I am more and more convinced that I will be simply deported to Guinea, like a mere native, as happened to Cordeiro da Matta after his argument with Cid Baptista. They are going to treat me like a savage to whom modern laws refuse any right - even the right to humanity -, my situation being worsened by the fact that they consider me a subversive, dangerous element for the Cazengo and Ambaca districts, where I supposedly incited the savages to the massacre of Europeans! (*Relato* 2 13-14).

Assis Júnior's bitter irony really seems to rule out any violent intention. In the first volume of Relato dos Acontecimentos de Dala Tando e Lucala the author also explains his real feeling about the independence of Angola. In his opinion 'independence' was the favorite word used by defenders of the statu quo in order to legitimate all kind of injustice, theft and cruelty inflicted on an overseas people, even if the constitution theoretically ensured political equality and rights to all the monarchy's subjects:

> But the Fundamental Law is torn off anytime it is convenient for the men in charge (...) The idea of independence does exist, it is true, but it only exists in the imagination of plotters accusing placid citizens of being the leaders of armed revolts; it exists in the

minds of those who would not allow the colonies to develop and hold them in captivity, preventing the people from any access to education and prosperity, worried by the idea that an intellectually developed and prosperous country would inevitably claim self-governance (...) it exists in the minds of who cannot adapt to the spirit of our century, those who demand blind, slave-like obedience for their fellow citizen, a kind of obedience which disgraces and humiliates mankind and therefore causes the people to revolt. Where righteousness dwells, the existence of a native uprising – a revolution– is deliberately invented. Because the black man never can be right. (*Relato 1* 36)

Much more than simply denouncing the events occurring in the country, Assis Júnior's work also provides the characterization of African people as citizens whose rights had been violated. As far as civil and political rights are concerned, African characters are placed on the same universal plan of the white man's world, but they are forced to play the role of a sociological minority in the face of the Europeans, the sociological majority imposing its rule. According to the point of view of a 'civilized native' such as Assis Júnior, the concept of civilization could not be merely explained by the overused dualities 'civilized versus uncivilized' or 'modernism versus archaism': ideally speaking, 'civilization' was synonymous with modernity regardless of racial categories and cultural identities. As suggested by the Portuguese historian, Fernando Augusto Albuquerque Mourão, in this context modernity was not synonymous with European culture, and even less with the white settlers' culture: even if the white man introduced the concept and remained its tangible sociological reference, the true meaning of modernity overstepped its actor and emerged as the outcome of a mutual dialectical involvement (*Mourão* 53-54).

Assis Júnior immediately understood that the patronizing assertions promoted by the establishment in Angola acted as a justification and an attempt at concealing abuses committed by the colonizers: "how can they affirm that our metropolis - of which Angola is a prolongation - ensures the most peaceful, gentle and humanitarian treatment to the natives, when the most civilized inhabitants of its colonies are needlessly martyred and sacrificed to their enemies' insanity?" (*Relato* 2 33). As a matter of fact, by the 1920s the potential opposition of the Angolan urban elite had been wiped out.

Beyond the grudges and conflicts of interest originated by the coexistence of different classes and social groups within the colonial hierarchy, an undeniable cause of tensions among some sectors of the Luanda Luso-African elite was its implacably increasing loss of privileges. Even if the situation urged the closure of ranks against any threat to the group's social stability, a progressive deterioration of life conditions enhanced individual competition, especially amongst holders of the same office. Issues related to family hegemony, professional competition, personal enmities caused by 'treasons' or ambiguous attitudes towards the authorities -as clearly described by Paixão Franco in História de uma traição- were also quite common.

Different cultural practices corresponded to different statuses that depended on the system's patterns of organization, hierarchy, prestige, segregation and so on. In the same way, the inclusion in a rural or urban environment more or less distanced from the centres of power provided individuals with different opportunities, independently from their skills or professional and political expectations. With their primary goal and object of consensus lying in the preservation of their hegemony over the colony, the native sons of the land unsurprisingly developed conflicting and contradictory tendencies and positions which resulted in the impossibility of articulating an alternative political project to Portuguese rule.

As a consequence of the intentional lack of commitment to public education displayed by the metropolis, the urban elite was progressively excluded from colonial administration to be substituted by freshly arrived Portuguese settlers. Once deprived of the chance to print journals and newspapers, the native sons of the land were forced to limit their political struggle to the creation of self-founded cultural and mutual assistance associations that often could at most offer teaching courses to their associates. Their claims, however, often presented a combination of strongly contradictory positions. On one hand they harshly criticized the colonial administration, denouncing the abuses committed by some of its officers, but on the other they tended to take advantage of legal omissions and opportunities whenever they could. From the 1880s on, for instance, the regime of forced work supplanted slavery and many elements of that group assisted the Portuguese to establish and operate a network of recruitment centres throughout the colony. In addition, it goes without saying that local farmers and landowners heavily relied on these exploited workers.

Finally, the constantly reaffirmed distinctions between different groups and the wide distance separating the urban elite from the rest of the native population prevented the formation of concrete alliances founded on tangible plans and common projects aimed at overthrowing the colonial regime. The idea of a large scale native uprising was feared by the white settlers as much as by the majority of those who played a mediating role between their employers and the natives by performing their duties as tax collectors, bookkeepers, civil servants and administration clerks; farmers and accountants in plantations and agricultural enterprises; officers and soldiers of the colonial army.

In conclusion, the strategy patterns used by this elite - condemned to a progressive isolation from the central course of the colony's social system by its inability to build stable alliances with other sectors of the African society- resulted in a series of different effects that, as also observed by Aida Freudenthal, blocked the way to the mobilization of a real nationalist movement for three decades (*Freudenthal* 572).

# Chapter 6

## *Violence as Metaphor*

D.Sanyal

A GOOD many writing from Africa have drawn quite heavily from oral literary traditions of the ancestral land. As Amos Tutuola and Chinua Achebe did prove since the publication of *The Palm Wine Drinkard* and *Things Fall Apart* in 1952 and 1958 respectively, the storytelling tradition of teaching and entertainment is an ancient bond linking the African bard with his communal land. This also marked a trend in the rating of postcolonial writings from the continent from the polarity of traditional oral to that of Euro-modern methods of literary craftsmanship. Surprisingly when Ekwensi's *People of the City* was published in 1954 it was acclaimed the first major novel in English by a West African to be widely read throughout the English speaking world. It was also touted with the promise to remain "a work of great significance in the development of contemporary African writing" ("People"1). This is in spite of various literary arguments "borne by the desire to articulate a specifically African aesthetic" ("African"1).

By the end of the twentieth century, however, there had grown a strong literary movement toward graphology of the struggle of the continent with colonialism, capitalism, as well as the devastation of ethnicity, war and unremitting despotism of indigenous rulers. These have been inscribed in Africa's modern existence using reestablished traditional tools of artistic pedagogy.

Given the present turmoil in African history it will not be improbable for postcolonial Nigerian artistes to continue the traditional role of the artiste as the voice of the people. And so have the early manifestation of protest in the novels, plays and poetry of Nigerian authors from Cyprian Ekwensi through Chukwuemeka Ike, Flora Nwapa, Isidore Okpewho, and Buchi Emecheta crystallised, a few years later, in fervid political cum traditional consciousness as being said of the works of writers such as Ben Okri and Chin Ce, to mention but two of the leading contemporary users of tradition and politics in modern fiction. Their respective works, *The Famished Road* (1991) with its "provocative and hopeful vision of the (African) world" (Blurb) and *The Visitor* (2004) that "challenges our linear view of time" (Blurb) highlight the grim confrontation of African tradition and modernity through the artistic combination of realism and fantasy. However the realism of Chin Ce's *Gamji College* story (2002) goes further to illustrate a metaphorical violence that is cyclical, unremitting and corporately vicious for Nigeria's spatial existence.

This reading will demonstrate that in Ce's prose fiction have been inscribed many vivid images of the postcolonial violence that have modern African states like Nigeria in a vice grip. The Nigerian national violence is as brutal to the psyche of individuals as it is to the state, and is perennially threatening to consume the national cultural and political ethos of the entire African region. It is also our premise that while *Gamji College* in a larger artistic perspective may deal with the character of the nation states of Africa under the various civilian and military regimes that govern them in the twentieth and twenty-first centuries (Brown par 1), its oral metaphors of violence are rendered in a manner that few recent fictional narratives in that African subregion have attempted. The overall interest of this study is therefore the story-teller's conceptualisation of violence, and how it envelopes his narrative, characterization and language in a way that brings out his message in its glaring -and uneasy- entirety.

The further appeal of *Gamji College* is seen in its "racy" pattern of dialogic inscription and a vision that is worthy of its own redemption. Through all of these, the metaphorical pattern of Gamji violence becomes, in extension, an exhumation of old and current socio-political problems of the nation in so far as African art presumes active partnership with historians and sociologists in the examination of human behaviour or social reality. In the Gamji story, the author significantly focusses on the youths of Africa in order to explain the "implications of the drift to anarchy on the intellectual and moral well being of the young ones" (Brown par 1). And here, as Hamilton rightly observes, Chin Ce's vision is similar to, although it goes beyond, that of Achebe's in its revolutionary, transformative potential. This is anchored on the objective of the story teller to, in Hamilton's perception,

> render visible all kinds of structures of
> subjectification by returning to history's lessons, to
> encourage a deep recognition and respect for others

and in so doing raise the potential for revolutionary activity at the hands of a socially and politically informed people. (104)

Thus in "cartograph(ing) the familiar anguish that surrounds the exclusion of African masses from the common wealth" the African chronicler of social history insinuates through his stories that "the low downs (must) recognize their limitations which lie in their scatteredness" especially where "leadership serves nothing more than mere consolidation of power" (Ogaga 172). In *Gamji College*, this idea is corroborated with characters who seem to be iconoclasts of the modern Nigerian dilemma. Says Marques in "The Works of Chin Ce: A Critical Overview,"

> just like Jerry and Tai seem to learn from observing the miseries of others, the reader too can learn from the display of mostly decadent situations, actions and poor or misinformed ways of thinking and perceiving reality. (16)

This process of learning via the methodology or direction of an experienced bard-craftsman would induce what Marques calls "the beginning of a cure" arising from "constant dialogue "between past, present and future" – the "fundamental recipe for a more accomplished post colonial nation" (18).

Ce's metaphorical story of an African nation in distress (*Gamji College*) is divided into three sections entitled the "The Cross", "The Bottle" and "The Gun". Each of these sections is as separate from the other as the characters in the stories are different. They are however serially linked as all the action takes place in the college, although at different times. With this arrangement, quite similar to the author's first published work, *Children of Koloko*, each of these stories, told through the viewpoint of three major characters, give us additional insights to, and empathy with, Ce's aggregate vision for the youths (college students) of Africa as a community of human beings whose actions would ultimately determine the destiny of their continent.

Fanaticism as Violence

The metaphor of religious fanaticism is clearly noticeable from the first section entitled "The Cross". Here the author seems to suggest that the nation's Ivory tower is, in popular Christian parlance, "the cross that it has to bear" in a modern transitional society. While the second story "The Bottle" focusses on the lack of direction among the youths as seen in their inebriation (drinking) and wildness of manners, the last section, "The Gun", is a metaphor of the violence and realpolitik in practice by Africa's political gladiators and their teeming supporters. All these are probable and real life portraiture of contemporary Nigerian society.

In "The Cross", awareness is drawn to a sinister and destructive form of violence that is rooted in national polity: an arrogant Pentecostalism -not exactly in the cavalier manner of Wole Soyinka's Jero. Christian evangelism seems to undermine most indigenous cultures and still threatens to confine Africa to the dustbin of the scientific world. The result is that Africa has become a continent perpetually imitating Europe's role models. As the story progresses we can see and identify the religious hypocrisy, fanaticism and intolerance that Gamji leaders have copied from their mentors in Europe and America. As soon as Tai, the major character, enters college, he is harassed by some religious converts seeking for new members to join their camp. James, a member of a Pentecostal fellowship, comes to his room to negotiate his allegiance to both God and man. And although he pretends he has come for his welfare, he immediately arranges for him to attend the newcomer's fellowship: "I am inviting you in Jesus name. Come and be blessed. After you must have had your rest of course..." (18). Tai agrees reluctantly. At the fellowship there is a curious mix of religion with politics. The national leader who graces the occasion because his nephew is the rector of the college uses the opportunity to canvass for support of his government. He attacks other opponents who do not support his fraudulent programmes. Tai seems unimpressed that religion is brazenly allied to politics in what is supposed to be a citadel of learning. Thus other times that James comes to take him to fellowship, he continues to offer apologies. The day comes when he summons courage to announce his lack of interest. He tells them they are hypocrites and that if the president was truly a man of God as claimed, then the college, i.e., the nation (Nigeria), should have earned a better place in history. Because he rejects this religious partnership, the brothers of the church, namely James and Peter, tell him he will go to hell fire: "Then the devil will have you!" Peter pronounced with vehemence..." (48). Here is a seemingly innocuous story but one which is profoundly significant in the way the author's draws attention to ordinary events of individual lives that have profound bearing on Nigerian and African history.

The Self Destructs of Modernity

There is the second important metaphor of confusion among the youths and this is found in the story of "The Bottle" which is a possible echo of Soyinka's The Interpreters. As the title of this second part suggests, the youths have hit the bottle and lost their sense of direction. This is easily seen in the actions of Femi, Dogo and Milord who are major characters of the story. Sitting in a crowded and noisy drinking parlour of the college premises, the students have plenty money to waste on the green bottle during the new session. There is a sign of waste in the excess of drinks that Dogo continues to order from Sammy, the bartender. Yet despite this profligacy, they also complain about their country and its corruption and ineffectual public services such as government-run electricity and media corporations.

In this story, Ce laces the dialogues between cronies and rivals with ironies: Femi is going to be a lawyer. Dogo is going to be a doctor. Milord is reading philosophy. It is left to the reader to discern if they can succeed with all the extroversion and inebriation as they exchange verbal cudgels such as: Dogo's people from the North put women in purdah in the name of religion and the Shah forbids drinking but Dogo probably drinks more than everyone. A drunken Milord is afraid to close his eyes because of the frightful vision he is beginning to imagine. The imperturbable three in their ferocity of shouting and argumentation continue their escapade until past midnight when everybody leaves the joint. These future leaders, as the story is at pains to portray them, are the last to leave the drinking hall. Of course this does not speak well of their future as Milord, one of the participants in the drama, seems to realise:

They were the last to leave, Milord noted with a
smile of amusement and a pang of guilt excepting,
reassuringly, the long their fellow slumped on the
seat by the far corner of the bar drooling away the
few hours. Before daylight. (71)

African Politics and Violence

The last story "The Gun" deals with the harsh tribal
intolerance and political violence that continue to dog
African postcolonial nations. The gun (violence) as the title
shows is the modern instrument to manipulate elections and
eliminate political adversaries. The major characters in this
story are Napoleon and Jerry. Gamji students' government
election is around the corner and everybody wants to run
for President. Even the church fellowship wants to have its
own candidate for President. The school authorities of
Gamji also want an "indigene" to be President and the
authorities are determined that the position never goes to a
"stranger", revealing that ethnic rancour, tribalism,
discrimination and violence are the basis of the new
postcolonial African co-existence.

Napoleon brazenly totes a gun and boasts that he will be
President by any means. Like any contemporary Nigerian
politician, Napoleon talks big, says a lot about revolution
and his mission to save the people. Jerry supports him
because he is his friend, although he knows Napoleon is not
the best candidate. At the night of campaign, there is a fight
between two opponents and there is a gunshot. This
violence carries over to the day of elections. But it is not a
free and fair election. There are lots of irregularities and
lack of discipline. More violence further mars the process:

125

Ege, one of the presidential candidates is killed in a shoot-out. Ege is presumed better than the rest for his public speeches so he is a natural target for political assassination.

Since the college of Gamji, like most African governments, cannot boast of free and fair elections except clandestine rigging and violent clashes the elections are cancelled. But before then Jerry is fed up with the killing and demonstrates this revolt by withdrawing his support of his friend. He is saddened by the shooting of Ege and understandably disappointed with the conduct of his peers, especially in the murder of a candidate in cold blood:

> ....no one really cared who killed Ege, even as the elections were dissolved for the wanton arts of violence that characterized them and even as the dogs of Gamji howled through the nights for the spoils of the game. The howling haunted Jerry's memory ever after. (113)

"The Gun" is the climax of the religious or bohemian extravaganza that preceded it, and marks, indeed, a sad ending for the story about the college of Gamji. However, in spite of the violence, there is still the message of hope seen in Tai and Jerry -characters who stand for a few cynical members of young people that refuse to be part of the general sickness of Gamji's violent declivity. Brown rightly notes that Tai stands for a few sceptical members of the younger generations that refuse to buy into the hype and deception that post colonial politics have wrought on the polity (par 4). However, in the words of Irene Marques, the real questions that Chin Ce seems to be asking are:

How does one maintain oneself adequately sober (informed and aware) so that one is capable of seeing one self as an agent capable of making and changing that very history? How do we have a clearer holistic and interdynamical understanding of history so that we can then pave the way for a more genuine and ethical society? (107)

The story teller appears to have provided this answer by the creation of realistic characters who, dogged by the debilitating circumstances of their birth and experience, nevertheless claim an independent thinking that is different from what Hamilton calls "state thinking"(96). Where the Nigerian state and their leaders are shown to be brutal, devious, and violent in their individualism, Ce's protagonists are eclectic, witty, sardonic and random. In the plot of randomness, too, *Gamji College* rejects a simple plot structure although some of the stories are straightforward and definitely of a linear plot development. A good example is the first story, "The Cross". It begins with Tai's first day at college, shows us how disappointed he is on his first day. Then we see him meeting James and other members of the campus fellowship. The story ends with Tai and James quarrelling and ending their acquaintance in mutual dismissal. However, in "The Bottle" and "The Gun", the plot movement convolutes, moving back and forward at random. By combining both linear and convoluted plot structures in the story, we have random accounts that involve other less significant lives and their behaviours in a small but intricate network of shared responsibilities. These accounts are rendered through the minds of major characters of each story as may be seen below in the case where Jerry refuses to submit to a kinsman's play of tribal solidarity.

> Talking about allegiance to root Jerry nearly reminded Zykes his last duty as a good townsman which shamed every member of Koyo Progressive Union of Gamji. The story, in short, was that Zykes wanted to please the dim-witted outgoing president of Gamji college government who dotted on a young Koyo beauty far above his intelligence... Zykes wanted to please his political godfather and called his townswoman out in the middle of a KPU meeting. Uche had dutifully obliged. Once outside, there was President Bamako in the official 504 Peugeot saloon. And this was Zykes' proposal: Uche should accompany them to town for an official reception party for a VIP's wife. (115-116)

Jerry's random thoughts and recollections provide sub plots and incidents that render the story complex as do Tai's and, occasionally, Milord's flights of fancy. Further, the system of symbolic representation in the use of private markers both in verse and prose forms, common with Romantic period writers (Abrams 209), has been part of Ce's aesthetic experiments in his novels and poems, earning him the appellation of a Romantic (Eke 123). In *Gamji College* Ce uses this technique to draw attention to ideas or things or situations that occur in the story. The story of "The Cross" is represented by the dangling cross in front of the college building. This cross has been damaged by erosion and left half-fallen in front of the college rector's office. It is the signal for the falling integrity of religion and the fact that something needs to be done about the religious tendencies that are encountered in the story.

In the second section, "The Bottle" Sammy's drawing of the bottle in his bar symbolises the rowdy misdirection of the youths of Gamji. In the drinking parlour, the barman has a large bottle decorating the joint. And on top of the bottle, he writes: "To the glory of the green bottle" (51). The third story, "The Gun", has Napoleon toting this symbol of modern African dereliction in violence, election rigging and serial political assassinations. The wooden carving of a rifle dangling from his waist as he delivers his manifesto is the ultimate harbinger of death for political opponents such as Ege.

Language as Violent Metaphors

Unlike the degeneration of quality of education which Ce laments in his essay "Bards and Tyrants" about "Nigerian tertiary institutions (that) turn out graduates and teachers who … reel out clichés reminiscent of the hip hop of American backstreets" (12), the language of *Gamji College* characters is rather bombastic, although not deficient, for college students. A character like Dogo speaks imperiously of "bounteous patronage" (44) and "scientific misjudgment" (43); Milord thinks that Dogo's "diametrical sensitivity to tobacco was a paradox that his friends never really understood" (56). The incidence of bombast might indicate the story's thrust as dialectic of modern social conditions. Another point of the language of the book is the use of dialogue and conversation. "The Bottle" truly is written in conversational style like a dramatic performance.

This intriguing experiment is only fitting for a short telling. Brown rightly observes that "The Bottle" story comprises

> dramatic discussions ...(by) a new generation of young Nigerian African people who critique their environment and celebrate drunkenness and amnesia... as protest against a nation state that can no longer guarantee their future as its citizens. (par 1)

Further in language and characterization, Ce employs many characters of eloquent bearing not quite in the typical fashion of short story writing. Here each character seems to play his/her part and leave the stage. It is however glaring that these characters are pitched in an aggressive and vicious game consonant with the author's perception of a wobbling Nigerian state and its dribbling political chieftains. In "The Cross" we have Tai who is fighting or struggling with some members of the church fellowship such as James. The movement patterns after a violent, psychological struggle between Tai and James to say 'yes' or 'no'. In the words of the narrator, "sometimes it unnerved Tai. In spite of all attempts to retain his balance in this cat-and-mouse game, he wasn't succeeding" (38). Thus James keeps coming and praying for Tai's induction in the fellowship while Tai struggles against the prospect. This continues, cat-and-mouse fashion until Tai decides to end it for good.

> Tai's reaction in that instant was akin to their rage but somehow he tried to hold a grip on his emotions. He was not quite successful. His mind ached to spill out the bottled repugnance he had felt at this whole chicanery for the past weeks. (47)

In "The Bottle" too, the characters also play an aggressive hide-and-seek in which they trade verbal blames for their nation's myriad problems.

> Milord: Dogo you should know better traditions than that nonsense.
> Femi: Like burning down our drinking joints up North (guffaws) in the name of the shah.
> Dogo: (humoured) To sift the good from the bad. It's good for peace!
> Milord: Peace by lack of discipline?
> Dogo: Nonsense! Lack of discipline is your riots and cult practices. Criminality of culpable degree, you should know.
> Milord: And what of being drunk and noisy!
> Dogo (stout in defence): Drinking is a personal right! You can't take it away! (65-66)

The competition over who drinks more, or who takes the glory of the green bottle, is symptomatic of the competitive national experiment that Nigeria and many African nations have been mired in for too long in post-independence history. In the college Milord is first to get tired while Dogo claims the prize of the noblest drinker.

Finally in "The Gun", the contest is between Jerry, Napoleon and other contestants who struggle for power. Jerry, the journalist, records their movements and wiles as Napoleon battles for power with his gun. Ege who only has his mouth –the gift of the garb which is African-style politics of empty phraseologies– uses it very well on the manifesto night. But, with the heightening of the struggle for power, he is shot in a gun duel. The violence has grown chilling and the elections are cancelled to signal the end of a charade.

Violence as "Mirror"

Irene Marques sees in Ce's work the "mirror" effect present in various ways: the mirror of history via the use of overt or convert interdynamic historical representation and the mirror of character to character or character to reader (16). In her opinion,

> This multidimensional, didactic mirror as a narrative technique of major importance in Gamji College and also in several of Ce's other fictional or poetic works. By making use of this mirror by putting malaises on display and by showing the many agents and transhistorical agencies that are making the society the putrid pit it is the writer, like the doctor, is writing a complete and through chart, that becoming what Coetzee calls "the medical diagnostician of the state. (15-16)

The mirror of violence inscribed in every paragraph of the story stretches full gamut in this contemporary fiction as it does in the politics and social realities of modern Nigerian existence. *Gamji College* is thus a post-colonial narrative discourse that deals incisively and precisely with the realities of his society. Indeed *Gamji College* is truly a serious indictment of Nigeria's political leadership. This is evident in the portrayal of leaders such as Baba Sonja who use religion to hoodwink the masses and further their own selfish ends. By spotlighting upon "society and citizens who are disgusted with the conduct of black governments in a post colonial era" (Usongo 112), the story teller takes a hard look at the will of the younger generation of Nigerian youths who, having no sense of direction as a result of the confused leadership, must nevertheless strive to subvert all those agents of their social limitations. Thus the sum of the vision of the writer, being that something urgent needs to be done to Africa's social, political and educational institutions in order to remedy a serious problem in the continent, is executed by the novel employment of complex and simple sequences, oral metaphors, symbolism, and "mirror" effects of narration. In a story, Ce has dealt diverse and suitable narrative justice to a modern African reality.

# Chapter 7

## *Representing Conflict, Imagining Consensus*

O.A.Ayinde

WE shall examine the category of conflict in Khālid Ibrāhim 'Uways' novel *al-Ruqs taht al-Matar* (Dance under the Rain, 2001). Unlike Tayyeb Şālih whose forte largely inheres in his iconic portrayal of the interface between the Sudanese and the colonialist, 'Uways' is *sui generis* in its attention to the inner schisms in the post-independence Sudanese society particularly the seemingly unending North-South interface, the violent racial conflict between the black- and Arab-Sudanese, the inscription and circumscription of gender by nationalism and the overall shifting identities of postcolonial Sudanese modernities. Central to this study is the exploration of how inter-racial/cultural and intra-racial /cultural trajectories in Sudan have served as an impulse for creativity and how the latter, in turn, hacks back to the very reality from which it derives its origin and strength.

In searching for "meaning" in *Dance*, therefore, we pay attention to a combination of African, Eastern and Western critical styles including Abdul Qāhir al-Jurjāni, Adonis, Edward Said, Jean-Paul Sartre, Chinua Achebe and Frantz Fanon. How have the dialectics and the plethora of conflicts in Sudan impacted Sudanese literature and what knowledge do they vouchsafe for Africa in its attempt to make sense of itself and its future? How has Sudanese literature mirrored the racial, gender and national fissures and frictions in contemporary Sudan and what cultural cue does it yield for the country in its effort at building consensus among its citizens? What other perspectives, aside from the sociological and political, could characters we read about in Sudanese literature, particularly in *Dance*, furnish with reference to intra-Sudanese conflicts and how might we, using al-Jurjāni's thesis on "intellectual" (al-ilmī) and "imaginative" (al-takhayulī) meanings in literature, describe them?

To talk about the category of conflict in the Sudanese novel might not satisfy Edward Said's thesis to the effect that "every novel is a form of discovery" (82). This is because conflict, with respect to al-Sūdān, is the Zeitgeist1 - the spirit of the age. As a historical construct, the Sudan, since the medieval to the modern period, has been a locale for contests and conflicts between and among disparate ethnic communities and, in the words of Ali Mazrui, "the multiple marginalities" (240-255) that inhabit its rigid terrain. As a post-modern/colonial site, the geographies of the Sudanese landscape is presently being shaped, no more by "multiple marginalities" but "multiple complexities" (Ahmed 71) of the Sudanese subjectivities. As a cultural problematic, the category of conflict in the Sudan continues to defy the simplistic binary between good and evil and between Northern and Southern Sudan. Rather the country has the enviable (?) record, at least with reference to Africa, of being one in which conflict exists, on the one hand, between the 'black' and the 'white', and, on the other, among the 'white,' the 'black' and the neither 'white' nor 'black.' As if by compulsion, the Sudan celebrates the uncanny union of the real, the farcical and the absurd; it is a site where conflict is the nodus of being; it is a space where conflict is the driving force of existence.

Now, if the subject matter of conflict has become so intertwined, quite paradoxically, with the very essence of the Sudanese nation, then its appropriation by imagination must necessarily be for purposes other than mere re-presentation of its dynamics. In other words, in order for the novel to be relevant in postcolonial Sudan, it should most likely set for itself the task of, in the words of Chinua Achebe, "re-educating" complex Sudanese subjectivities and "regenerating" (103) Sudanese cultural values. Put differently, the Sudanese novel that would titillate the Sudanese literary appetite and, therefore, merit our attention should be such as would satisfy, in line with Edward Said, the urge in humanity "to modify reality" (82a). Ahmad Muhammad al-Mahjūb graphically pictures this when, writing in the 1930s in Sudan, he says: "what's the essence of literature if it does not assist people on revolution and change in life…and in propelling…(the people) on to the current of progress and development?" (13).

Thus in Uways' *Dance under the Rain*, we shall examine how the novel attempts "to modify reality" in Sudan through its representation of the topoi of conflict in the country. In order to achieve the foregoing, however, it is important for us to examine intra-Sudanese existential/ historical/ cultural valences that accentuate conflict in

Sudan before its appropriation by Sudanese writers. In other
words, the starting point of an inquiry into the category of
conflict in the Sudanese novel, and one in which the motifs
of race, gender and nationalism are embedded, should be an
investigation, albeit briefly, of the extremely charged field
which spawned racial, gender and national consciousness in
Sudan before its appropriation by Sudanese writers. Thus,
the following question becomes extremely urgent: what
could be the fountain(s) for the conflictual identities of the
Sudanese in the contemporary period and how might it be
useful in our attempt to understand the problematics of race,
gender and nationalism in the Sudanese novel? In
answering these questions the probing statements of the
renowned Sudanese writer, al-Tayyib Ṣāliḥ, compels our
contemplation. Writing in al-Majallah close two decades
ago, al-Tayyib Ṣāliḥ says:

> One of the reasons why this country is always in
> turmoil could be attributed to the fact that its name
> means nothing to its people. What is Sudan? Egypt is
> Egypt, Yemen Yemen, Iraq Iraq and Lebanon
> Lebanon. But what is the Sudan? We have continued
> to trundle on with this hollow colonial legacy. (137)

These statements from al-Tayyib Ṣāliḥ are of high
importance to any analysis of the problematic of conflict in
Sudanese culture. The statements essay a reasoned gulf
between the Sudanese and his/her nation. They portray the
former in a state of angst, utterly disoriented with
him/herself and completely disenchanted with the very first
element that defines his/her identity: al-Sūdān. Specifically
the question, 'what is Sudan?' mirrors the Arab-Sudanese's
rejection of al-Sūdān. The name is rejected probably

because it effaces, in line with Ibn Khaldun's thesis, "the historicity" of the Arab-Sudanese "as an historical group" (qtd. in Al-Azmeh 38). al-Sūdān 'inflicts' 'blackness' on the latter; with it, the most important critical factor for national cohesion and identity formation in Sudan becomes circumscribed by colour: blackness[2].

The rejection, by the Arab-Sudanese, of al-Sūdān does not, however, mean the celebration of the name by the black-Sudanese. This is because the circumscription of nation by colour and the inscription of Sudan with the black identity have not, since the early modern period, led to any improvement in the socio-political and economic realities of the black-subjects in Sudan. Throughout the period of the British hegemony over the Nile Valley and years after Sudanese political independence extreme and, perhaps, deliberate under-development of the Southern and Western parts of the Sudan, both of which represent the bastion of black identities in the country, has continued[3]. For example during the British rule "only four government primary schools" (Prunier 26) could be found in the whole of Dar Fur. Schools and other educational facilities were and have not been provided in these areas probably based on the fact that, in line with George Antonius, "without school or book" (Antonius 40) the yearning for a nation by the black-Sudanese would be inconceivable. Thus while the Arab-Sudanese is in conflict with al-Sūdān because of 'race'/colour, the black-Sudanese, on the other hand, rejects it because of its empty promises as a 'nation'.

The foregoing only represents a perspective, however. In other words, it is not only colour/race and nation that have informed the epistemology of conflict in postcolonial Sudan, lack of consensus over gender role(s) has also served as an important fountain for conflict, frictions and fissures among Sudanese citizens. From the farthest regions of southern Sudan to its northern peripheries, arguments abound not only over the essence of the male or female in nature but also what socio-cultural and political space(s) could be yielded to each in the Sudanese construction of its identity. Within this gender spectrum, however, the Sudanese woman is usually at the receiving end. She has no independent identity. She usually watches as her body is, in the words of Muhsin al-Musawi, "confiscated, sold out, drawn upon, mapped and deprived of its own identity" (al-Musawi 223). During the pre-independence era[4] her body was a contested site between the colonist and the colonized. In the post-independence period, her identity has again been appropriated and invaded by the conflictual subjectivities in Sudan in their inter-racial and intra-national and cultural transactions; on her body the North and the South violently intersect. She is the "necessary allegorical ground for the transaction in national history" (Radhakrishnan 77).

Contrasting the figure of the woman with the man in Sudanese culture yields interesting images for us to behold. Without attempting to explore in-depth how he has been "produced" culturally,[5] the male in Sudan may be categorized into to three: al-rajul (the male), nisfu al-rajul (half male, read the effeminate), and al-rajul al-kāmil (complete male). The complete male in Sudanese Arab-Islamic culture, for example, is not only the opposite of the female but is the quintessential "spermatic animal per excellence" (Foucault 112). It is with reference to him that the patriarchates have divided authorities in nature into two: the one in heaven and the other on earth; "to God belongs the powers in the heaven; to the ... (complete male) belongs the power on earth" (Wadi 271). At the inter-gender level the complete male is a warrior: the conqueror of the female.

At the intra-gender level, men in Sudanese cultural hierarchy acquiesce, either by choice or compulsion, to his authority. Thus the gender problematic, in addition to that of race and nation, could, therefore, be seen as the doxa – the dominant issues in contemporary Sudanese life. They constitute, in a contrapuntal manner, "the ideas, the concepts and the experience" (Edward Said(b) 73) from which the Sudanese novel draws support. It is to its portrayal and the representation of its trajectories in Sudanese culture that 'Uways novel, Dance, is dedicated.

Narrated by the author, Dance tells the story of Stephen Michael Donato, the hero, J'afar, 'Umar, Nafīsah, Robert John Kolant and Tony. Even though the hero and Robert are from Southern Sudan, they are friends to J'afar, Umar, Abdul Gani, Nafīsah, all of whom are Arab-Sudanese. Both J'afar and Nafīsah are children of a medical doctor by name Muhammad Ahmad while Tony, the Southerner, is their house-servant. Apparently born after the attainment of independence by Sudan, all the characters, excepting Robert and Nafīsah – both of whom are students in the law of school – became friends when they met in the Sudanese Military College. Their parents wanted them to pursue such fields of human endeavour as medicine and law but they chose to go for military training probably to mirror the condition of the postcolonial Sudanese nation: a nation at war itself; a nation constantly on the brink of an implosion. Aside from these characters there is Muhammad Ṣālih, the Arab-Sudanese elderly house-assistant to the hero, Stephen Michael Donato.

Dance has two beginnings: one in the South and the other in the North of Sudan. The first conduces to the metaphysical patrimonies and cosmogonic sensibilities of the hero, the second images post-independence Sudanese socio-political landscape; the first attend to the hero's Southern origin, identity and reminiscences, the second patronizes his trials and travails in northern Sudan; the first patronizes symbols and traditional cues in Southern Sudan, the second is sui generis in its portrayal of the rigid realities of modern Sudanese life in the North; the first mirrors how the hero, as a young village-boy, goes out into the bush very early in the morning only for him to "return as a grown-up child in his twenties" (8), the second is picaresque of how he departs Northern Sudan as a nationalist in search of his "nation." We shall delay the engagement with the symbolic in our reading of Uways' novel for the pragmatic, in line with the Arab axiom that every ending naturally returns to its beginning.

The pragmatic and the mimetic in Dance begin when the hero, Stephen Michael Donato, the Southerner, decides to go for a wedding feast organized by his friend in Umdurmān. Walking steadily as if on a mission, his hands in his pocket, he is seen by a group of young boys who had been playing on the street under the shining moonlight. His appearance immediately catches the attention of the boys. One of them exclaims, "Look at this black slave!!" (8). When a Southerner is seen in the northern parts of Sudan, his/her presence occasions an inner conflict in the xenophobic Northerner; the racialist alarm in the psyche of the latter automatically rings. His emotion is full of contempt and hatred for the black subject. The boys, three in all, thereafter walk up to the hero. One of them confronts him thus: "We are in need of a servant who will take care of our house!!". The second says: "Would you accept to work with us...The work is not difficult...cleaning of the house and utensils and laundry...we shall give you money that suits your service" (9). These statements are reminiscent of

141

a perspective in the dialectic image of the black-African as constructed both by the Arab-African writers and their counterparts in sub-Sahara Africa[6] which essays the black subject as an entity whose essence inheres in slavery and servitude. The statements made by the boys also call attention to the possibility of the continued incidence of slavery in the post-independence Sudan; the possibility, in line with John Eibner, that the "Sudan is the only place (in the contemporary period) where chattel slavery is not just surviving but experiencing a great survival" (Eibner 6). Instead of responding to these inflammatory comments, the hero decides to keep his calm. But his silence and sturdy posture only infuriates the boys the more. The hero, therefore, calmly says: "I have a job already, can I go please?" But the boys appear unprepared to let him have things his way. One of them then says: "Bring your mother instead!" (10).

By saying "Bring your mother instead" the boys, who, in the words of Bakhtin, could be referred to as "centripetal forces" operating in the midst of Sudanese "heteroglosia" (272) want to infuriate the hero; they desire to transform the texture of the conflict from the verbal to the violent. This is because in typical African societies, mothers are sacred entities -they are revered as the source of life and living[7]. Thus in instances when mothers are ridiculed, it is expected that their children should rise up and defend their honour. But rather than trying to redeem his mother's honour, the hero pleads with the boys once again to let him go saying: "I'm on my way to a wedding party, please let me go" (Uways 10). But the boys would not let him have things his way probably because the North-South interface thrives only when it becomes violent. Thus the hero seeks recourse to his professional training: he engages the three in physical combat. Violence occurs in the text as an effect, the cause being the refusal of the black subject to remain where he is put by the Other; the refusal of the Southerner to carry the can of guilt; the sturdy refusal of the black subject to profess and confess his inferiority. A police officer soon emerges unto the scene. He asks the boys what went wrong. In unison they chorus: "It is this hopeless Southerner…he is trying to rob us" (10). The policeman does not think twice before saying: "O! these Southerners would cause nothing but trouble…follow me to the station" (10). Here reference to the hero, neither as a black man nor a slave, but a Southerner means the word is the third variable in the polyglot; the third in the panoply of adjectives usually employed by the Northerners in reference to their compatriots from the South. The employment of the word "Southerner" enjoys plausibility not only because it is a racial concept but also because it affirms the political binary in Sudan: the North/South, Muslim/Christian and Arab/non-Arab divide. In the reckoning of the Northerner, the Southerner is "primarily a non-Northerner" (al-Effendi 372) the same way the Northerner is primarily a non-Southerner. This political game denies the possibility and in fact the reality that not all Southerners are Christians nor are all Northerners Muslims. It also refuses to instantiate the fact that not all Northerners are Arab (white) and that not all Southerners are black. When it becomes clear to the hero that he is being seen as the perpetrator, not the victim of racialism by the agent of government – the police, he reaches for the inner chest of his pocket and brings out his identity card. This achieves the desired result. The police officer discovers that the hero is an officer in the military and begins to plead out of fear and humiliation saying, "Sorry sir! You can go" (Uways 10). The hero eventually arrives J'afar's house. There he meets his friends and associates all of whom seek to know the reason for his late arrival to the party. The hero's response is brisk and terse: "a small problem on the way" (11).

A couple of days thereafter the hero pays Robert a visit on campus. He enters a canteen, requests for a hot cup of tea and awaits the arrival of Robert who joins him. A short while thereafter, the hero catches sight of Nafīsah, the younger sister of his friend, J'afar, who is also engaged in a conversation with her colleague by name Rashid. A short while after the exchange of pleasantries between the two, the hero goes back to his friend, Robert. He has hardly taken his leave when he hears Rashid whisper to Nafīsah: "Who could this slave be?" Nafīsah replies: "He is one of the friends of J'afar!!" Rashid then says coldly: "Is it that your brother can't find the free born he could pick as friend?" (21)

Although Rashid says this silently he fails to reckon with the possibility that in the conflictual terrain which Sudan has become, in the racialist spaces of Khartūm and Umdurmān and one in which the black subject is, in the words of Frantz Fanon, "over-determined from without...dissected under the white eyes" (Wretched 116), the hero's "antennae" would "pick up the catch phrases" (116) of racialism as soon as they are let loose by the racialist. In other words, apart from the guilt complex, conflict ensues in and outside the text in Sudan for "psycho-affective" (40) factor -a factor which operates in the temporal spaces occupied by the racialist and the racialized subject in the country. In other words, the affectivity of the racialist and racialized subjects in Sudan is constantly on "edge like a running sore flinching from a caustic agent" (50). The hero would not let such derision and demeaning comments from Rashid pass without seeking redress. He goes back to the spot where Nafisah and her friend are sitting but only finds Nafisah who is completely engrossed in a book. He then goes on to confront her thus: "I regret the fact that you are reading law!" ('Uways 23). Nafisah opens her eyes wide in utter confusion and humiliation especially when she realizes that the statement is directed to no other person other than herself. The two characters, thereafter, engage each other in a confrontation:

> "Nafisah! Have you learnt in law that human beings are in categories based on their colour and skin? What kind of law would that be?
>
> Nafisah looks the hero straight in the face and retorts saying:
>
> "Listen Sergeant Michael, you have your world and we have ours!
>
> "I'm not a slave to anybody, Nafisah! I was created black by God, but he has not left in me any seed of stupidity and insignificance…my ears caught the conversation between you and your friend a while ago and I felt blood rush to my veins. I nearly returned to slap his ugly face…" (23)

Days after the confrontation between the two, Nafisah's mind remains fixed on the encounter. In the night she stays awake. Images of the hero and their hot exchange occupy her heart. She is particularly disturbed by the challenges the hero posed to her and his interrogation of her identity and world-view. Being an Arab-Sudanese and daughter of the rich she shares the anti-South/black sentiments of the North. She sees the black-Sudanese as an evil. She says to herself: "…nothing is worse than these (black) people!!" (25). She begins to contemplate the ideals that the hero stands for: "Stephen desires to change the order of nature! Never! Perhaps he thinks...he could (in reality) be counted as one of us..." (27). Here "the order of nature" references the privilege which the 'white' enjoys in ruling and running over the 'black'. By saying "...he thinks...he could be counted as one of us..." Nafisah also invites reminiscences of Frantz Fanon's sharp analyses of life in the colony: "...what divides this world is first and foremost what species, what race one belongs to" (xx). Thus post-independence Sudan becomes a replica of the British-Sudan. In the former the Sudanese authorities become postmodern colonialists; the black subjects become postmodern colonized subjects. But the encounter between the hero and Nafisah dramatically functions in establishing a relationship between the two. Both characters eventually move from conflictual /adversarial postures to that of consensus and mutual respect; from mutual respect to affection. Nafisah begins to adore the hero's masculinity, intellectuality and uncanny perspectives to life; the latter, in return, starts to appreciate her preparedness to rediscover herself; her preparedness to discover the solemn and profound knowledge of the world wherever it may be found. Thus gender-racial conflict, in Dance, is conceived.

In Aristotle's thesis conflicts sometimes ensue in human societies based on, among others, disproportionate growth of one part of a city in comparison to the other, the adversarial interface between the poor and the rich and the contest between justice and injustice (Bickford 398-421)[8]. Tony, the house servant, the hero and other Southern Sudanese would probably have remained in Southern Sudan had it been the case that basic necessities of life have been more equitably distributed by the authorities. Thus when the

Southerner comes to the north, s/he does that not as a tourist but in search of living; in search of, in Aristotelian parlance, 'profit'. Once s/he arrives the North, the latter ceases to belong only to the Northerners. Rather the North becomes, de facto, a no-man's land.

Thus the hero derives confidence in protecting the young Tony. In doing that, however, he achieves two things in the text: the establishment of black consciousness in the face of white affirmation, not the creation, of an uncanny solidarity between the working class as a counterpoise for the oppression of the ruling class. The solidarity that exists among the working class, the oppressed and the poor in Sudan is instantaneous; it precedes the oppression of the oppressors; it is innate and immanent, not acquired and contingent like that among the rich. By saying "You aren't god by virtue of your being white", the hero is affirming the truth of black consciousness which gains strength in the same way that "the truth of the ruling-class consciousness", in line with Fredric Jameson's thesis, "is to be found in working-class consciousness" (290). Yet the statement "You aren't god by virtue of being white" still raises a number of questions. What makes an Arab-Sudanese "white" in relation to the Black-Sudanese but "black" in relation to the British? Is reference to the Arab-Sudanese as "white" either by the Arab- or the black-Sudanese valid? Is the "white" subject truly white like snow or common salt? These questions are pertinent not only for their relevance to any discourse which concerns itself with the categories of race and nation, but also for our attempt to make sense of postcolonial intra-African relations. Thus by saying "you aren't god by virtue of being white", the hero appears to be desirous of separating colour from status; he seeks to deconstruct the age-long notion which equates blackness with evil and whiteness with goodness and virtue. The hero seeks to establish the humanity of all Sudanese in order to dismantle the "modern day colonialism" (Uways 28) in his country; in order to place the Sudanese on a socio-political and social spectrum where equality and justice would be the touchstone of intra-social and inter-communal relations.

But the hero would soon discover the reality and the elasticity of racialism in Sudan. He is accused of being responsible for Nafīsah's refusal to marry Rida, the choice of her family. He is visited by his friend J'afar who asks him: "Sergeant Michael, tell me what's between you and Nafīsah." The hero contemplates his friend and says: "Nafīsah is my friend and sister O! J'afar. I have great feelings of respect and honor for her...I haven't entered your house with the intention to dishonor it" (59). But J'afar has ceased being a friend to the hero. He retorts: "Dog...you dishonorable negro, if you go near her, I would shatter your head with bullets, listen ...She is going to marry Rida in a weeks time...do you hear me? (59). By calling the hero a dog, J'afar employs what is known in Arabic rhetoric as Kināya. Kināya is a rhetorical trope which, according to the medieval Arab critic, Abdul Qāhir al-Jurjāni, is "a meaning which you comprehend not by way of the word(s) used, but by way of the meaning expressed" (Dalāil al-'Ijāz 330). Thus the description of the hero as a dog is with a purpose: J'afar desires to attribute to him the notions of bestiality and inhumanity that are ordinarily inherent in a dog. Dogs, in Arab-Islamic culture, are not fit as human companions; at best they are employed in games and hunting. His reference to the hero as a 'dog' also travels the familiar track in modern Sudanese narrative discourse in which the black subject is given series of names and adjectives all of which portray him as depraved and an irrational being. Thus when reference is made to the black subjects such as Kilāb al-Mas'ūrah (Mad Dogs), Adawāt mawt al-Sawdāh (Black Instruments of Death), Thīran Āijah (Violent Bulls) and Dhamāu li al-Dimā (Blood Thirsty)9 we are awakened to racial politics in the text; we are reminded of the politics and poetics of colour in Sudanese culture; we feel impelled to engage the problematic of race as it appertained to Sudan in earnest. Thus we begin our return journey to the beginning in Dance.

Racial Conflict

In reading specifically for "race" we begin with the symbolic: the role of blood in the construction of the epistemology of race in Sudan. The hero remembers having asked his father once: "My father, do you hate the Arabs?" But the old man refrains from offering an immediate answer to the hero's question. Rather he picks up a broken bottle and makes an incision on his arm. Then the following dialogue ensues between the two:

> "What's this Stephen?"
> "Blood"
> "What's its colour?"
> "Red"
> Then the old man says as follows: "Every child of Adam is created by God with a red blood, this is the origin, then he created for them different colours."
> (20)

Here blood becomes a signifier: the signified being the primordial equal status of the human race. Here, again, colour becomes secondary and arbitrary: its employment as a standard in measuring human quality and in bestowing honour and privileges becomes arcane, invalid and an infringement on divine wisdom. In Southern parts of Sudan, the human blood is held to be sacred. To share the same blood group is to share the same racial identity; to share the same cultural traits; to carry the same genetic codes from which proceed evil and good. There in Southern Sudan, the Arab-Sudanese are seen to be as bad as the blood that runs in their veins. Thus the ordinary Southerner has the notion that the possibility of a union between the North and the South of the country is as remote as the union of the heaven and earth. Deng quotes one of them as follows: "The Northerner is a person you cannot say will one day mix with the Southerner to the point where the blood of the Southerner and the blood of the Northerner will become one" (191- 227). But *Dance* imagines this very possibility.

When the hero is accidentally shot in a military parade in the barrack and consequently hospitalized, he is told he would need blood transfusion for him to survive. Muhammad Ṣāliḥ, his Arab servant could not, because of his old age, be of help. The latter, therefore, goes from the east to the west of Umdurmān in search of blood donors all to no avail. Nobody is willing to come forward and save the life of the hero who is already in a state of coma. Eventually Nafīsah steps forward. She offers to provide the blood that would save the hero in return probably for the latter's effort in assisting her in her "search for self-validation" (Black 213). When the hero regains his consciousness, the first person he sees by his side is Nafīsah. She gets hold of his hand, places it in her palm and with a voice laden with love and compassion says: "I nearly died of fear over you!" The hero looks her straight in the face and exclaims thus: "Your blood is running in my veins!" (Uways 63).

Thus Nafīsah, the Arab-Sudanese and, the hero, from the South of Sudan, achieve that which is deemed ordinarily impossible by the Sudanese. Both characters overcome the cultural, not primordial, barriers between 'white' and 'black' in order to open new vistas in inter-racial space in Sudan. Both characters migrate from their 'whiteness' and 'blackness' in order to chart new directions for Sudan's fortune and destiny. The character of Muhammad Ṣālih further accentuates this perspective. Muhammad Ṣālih, the elderly servant to the hero is a Muslim and from the farthest parts of northern Sudan. He had previously served the Egyptian Pashas before coming to Sudan to work in the houses of the Sudanese notables. He even worked briefly for Nafīsah's family before he is asked to leave sequel to his old age. At the beginning, he refused to work for the hero. The latter once asked him "Why did you refuse to work for me initially?" Muhammad Ṣālih responds thus: "When my people ask me for whom are you working...I would say: a Southerner..! They would then burst into laughter and say: he has become a slave to a slave. (13)

But Ṣālih, the figure of the North -the image of the oppressor and the postcolonial racialist tendencies in Sudan, eventually agrees to work as a servant to the hero, the Southerner -the figure of the racialized and oppressed subjects in Sudan. This reversal of roles appears to partake of the contrarieties and paradoxes in the Sudanese cultural landscape. Sudan is the place where "the moon appears in the afternoon and the sun rises in the night; it is the place where the heavens send showers of fish and the fish in the ocean develop wings with which they fly in the skies" ('Uways 29).

Perhaps more importantly, the characters of Muhammad Ṣāliḥ, the hero and Nafīsah throw up the third category of race in Sudan for our contemplation: the Afrabians. The Afrabians, according to Ali Mazrui, represent that category in African culture which emphasizes the "interaction between Africanity and Arab identity and the possibility of a fusion between the two". (8). The Afrabians among the Sudanese, in line with Tayyeb Ṣāliḥ, prefer to see things "with three eyes, talk with three tongues" (Season 151) and relate to things as neither 'white', 'black' nor negroid. The characters of Muhammad Ṣāliḥ, the hero and Nafīsah, therefore, function in awakening the Sudanese imagination to the possibilities of the emergence of a consensus on the country's identities. They also serve in preventing our reading of race in Sudan from, in the manner of the postmodern, "being conclusive or teleological" (Hutcheon 8).

Conflict of Gender

What knowledge about gender does *Dance* furnish and how does it accentuate the conflictual spaces of the narration? How does the female see herself and the other? The female in this novel is represented by Nafīsah and the prostitute. Both provide two conflicting perspectives of gender for our contemplation. Nafīsah sees herself as a traditional woman who, even though she belongs to the upper class of the Sudanese society, believes her essence ontologically lies in her procreative ability. One night, before her relationship with the hero begins, she contemplates her own image and destiny. Nafīsah's notion of herself conforms to tradition: that women's place is in the home; not necessarily in the school nor in the offices10. The female in Nafīsah also considers herself incomplete in the absence of the male. This gives credence to Wadi's thesis to the effect that "everything is easy in the life of a woman except the man: he is the source of her conflicts and tribulations; he is the fountain of her happiness and sadness..." (Wadi 50)

But how do women see men in Sudan? The quintessential male, according to Nafīsah, is he with dreams and "means." The male of her choice is he with "good looks, lots of money and a beautiful car such that the hearts of the ladies should skip each time they see him" (Uways 26). In other words, the male of her dream should be materially comfortable. He should be such whose presence, as we have it in early Sudanese short stories, should lead to conflicts among the ladies over who should be his lover. This is, however, not the only perspective to heterosexual politics in Sudanese culture that we read of in the novel. The prostitute in one of the brothels in Umdurmān provides another perspective.

One night the hero pays a visit to the brothel. He meets the prostitute who welcomes him with excessive joy and happiness. She walks coquettishly in front him and, within a twinkle of an eye, begins to remove her night gown. As she does this she whispers lustfully thus: "O! I'm lucky tonight!! The female teacher, Safiyyah, used to say that Negroes are the most capable of all men on earth, I detest men who are soft!" (34) This statement reminds us of men's identity as constructed by Bint Majdhub in Tayyeb Ṣālih's Season of Migration to the North. According to her, a man's worth lies not in his ability to provide material comforts for his woman but in his ability to satisfy her in bed. In the presence of her son-in-law, Bint Majdhub confronts her daughter thus:

> "O! Amīnah this man has not denied you of any of your rights...your house is beautiful, your cloth is beautiful. He has also stuffed your hands and neck with gold. But it appears from his face that he is incapable of satisfying you on bed. Should you desire real sexual satisfaction I can introduce a man to you, if he comes to you he would not leave you until your soul breaks." (al-Tayyib(b) 80)

Women who share this notion of men see themselves as men's sexual plaything; as objects in the hands of men; as "the impalpable gate that opens into the realm of orgies, of bacchanals, of delirious sexual sensations" (Black Skin 177). They are also active bearers of the "look"; they look at men as sexual objects in the leitmotif of erotic spectacle.

But the foregoing does not necessarily lead to conflict in *Dance*. Gender conflict ensues in the text when Nafīsah begins to assert her agency through her refusal to marry the man her family has picked as her husband. She is immediately confronted by J'afar, her brother. The latter is the figure of the traditional Sudanese Afro-Arabic culture which sees the woman as an estate that belongs to the male. When he hears about her refusal to marry Rida, the choice of her family, blood rushes to his face. He considers her a threat: a threat against his masculinity. He also considers her refusal an affront against the patriarchal authorities as represented by his father. He therefore insists her sister would marry nobody else except Rida. Thus Nafīsah finds herself in conflict with her family when she decides to migrate, in the manner of Hassanah bint Mahmud in *Season of Migration to the North*, from the locale of the "female" to that of the "feminist"[12]; when she ceases being, in the words of Trinh Minha, the "made woman" (264) in order to become a woman in the making. Nafisah refuses the marital contract her family enters into with the family of Rida sequel to her discovery of the "new Nafisah" (63); she rejects Rida after having discarded the old Nafisah: the Nafisah "who has a veil on her heart and a covering on her intellect" (63). Her refusal to accept Rida implies an elaboration of oppositional discourse by the female; her rejection of the society's tradition which defines her as a thing to be possessed, a spoil of war. Thus the marriage is dissolved as soon as it is solemnized.

National Conflict

Still in the pursuit of the geographies of conflict in *Dance*, we come to the third in the categories we have identified, namely nation. What elements are constitutive of a nation? Using the theory of nation as evidence, Homi Bhabha proposes "the condition of belonging" (45) as fundamental to the emergence of the political entity known as a nation. But close to a century ago, the Arab congress, in 1913, made the following proposition:

> "In the view of political theorists, groups are entitled to the rights of a nation if they possess unity of language and of race according to the German school; unity of history and of tradition according to the Italian school; and unity of political aspiration according to the French. If we are to consider the case of the Arabs in the light of these three schools, we will find that they have unity of language, unity

155

of history and of traditions, and unity of political aspirations. The right of the Arabs to nationhood, therefore, finds endorsement in all schools of political theory." (qtd. in Nuseibah 49)

What the Arab Congress probably failed to take into consideration is the problematic known as al-Sūdān- a state which simultaneously and paradoxically enjoys that which it lacks: unity of history and tradition, unity of race, and unity of political aspiration. Al-Sūdān is like a magical pot. It constantly boils with Africanity, Arabicity and Arabfricanity. None of these Sudanese identities fathoms what the word nation means to the other. It is with reference to this problematic that the hero, the black-Sudanese, asks Nafīsah, the Arab-Sudanese, thus: "What's the idea of the nation with you?" ('Uways 22). Nafīsah looks the hero in the face without offering a response. She offers no response probably on the assumption that the hero is aware of the fact that as far as the ordinary Arab-Sudanese is concerned, the word "nation" means the Arab-Sudanese at war with the black-Sudanese. But in waging war against the black-Sudanese both the Arab- and black-Sudanese subjects are employed by the 'nation' in Sudan. This is represented by characters like 'Uthmān, a black-Sudanese and 'Umar and Mahmūd, the Arab-Sudanese. Despite the years he has put into the 'service' of his 'nation', 'Uthmān is arrested by the authorities on trumped charges of sedition and treason. He is accused of cooperating with insurgents in western parts of Sudan, probably Dar Fur, where new Sudanese subjectivities have emerged to redefine what it does mean to refer to Sudan as a nation and, perhaps more importantly, what it does mean to be a Sudanese. 'Uthmān is consequently "put in solitary confinement, then summarily

156

executed" ('Uways 39). Upon his death, his children become orphans; his family is forced to return "to their village in Western Sudan" (39).

The circumstance of the Arab-Sudanese in the Sudanese army is equally not better. 'Umar, returns from the war front and goes straight to the hero's house. Suddenly, he bursts into hot tears; his body starts to shake as if under a spell. The hero, assisted by Muhammad Ṣāliḥ, carries him into the inner room. After a while he stutters thus: "O! Stephen...scattered corpses...even flies wouldn't do what we did...my friend it was at the White Nile, we destroyed thousands without mercy..." (42).

The hero and Muhammad Ṣāliḥ begin to mourn the unfortunate Sudanese who have suffered the fate 'Umar has just painted. But the latter is not done yet. As if he is purging himself of his sins, he goes on to paint more pathetic details of the operation. 'Umar thereafter proceeds to resign from the army. He could not do what Mahmūd did at the battle front. The latter goes mad upon seeing the extent of the bloodshed and savagery the soldiers perpetrated. When he eventually regains his senses, he turns his gun on his forehead and shoots himself dead (44).

'Umar's story reminds the hero of the night in which his father was killed, sequel to the invasion of his village by the government forces. The story also brings images of his lost friends and close relations all of whom have either died in the violent conflict between the North and the South or have been permanently displaced. A couple of days after this incident, he also tenders his resignation from the army. The hero disengages from the army probably out of fear of losing, like 'Umar, his humanity; he disengages from the army as a nationalist in search of the 'nation' (73).

Conclusion

What has been done thus far is to grapple with meaning in *Dance*. Meanings, according to al-Jurjāni, are of two types: intellectual (aqlī) and imaginative -takhayilī (al-Balāgah 241). Intellectual meanings are "realized by reason and it is true for all people in all generations..." while "Imaginative meanings are those which cannot be said to be either true or false, nor can what it asserts be taken to be true or what it negates be taken as truly negative" (241). Using this proposition as our guide, and having the contours on the Sudanese political and cultural landscape under our focus, it could be argued that the meaning we derive from Dance is true, intellectual and objective. If, however, the characters and the conflicts in the novel are seen to be poetic and imaginary, the meanings we discern from the novel would then straddle the shifting topoi of truthfulness and falsehood. Whatever perspective we choose, it is axiomatic from this study that the Sudanese novel is, in the words of Jean Paul-Sartre, "in the midst of action fully engaged in ... (its) epoch" (Les Temps 1954)[11]. Its vocation includes the deracination of the Sudanese subjectivities, the promotion of more gender friendly society, and the construction of a nation where consensus would be the touchstone of intra/inter-national/communal relations.

# Notes and Bibliography

## Chapter 1
## Two Africas and the Writer

### Works Cited

Fanon, Frantz . *The Wretched of the Earth*. London: Penguin, 1967.

Kubayanda, J. B. "Dictattorship, Oppression, and New Realism." *Research in African Literatures, 21, 2.* Summer. Indiana University Press. 1990.

Larson, Charles R. *The Ordeal of the African Writer*. London and New York: Zed Books. 2001.

Larson, Charles R. "African Writers at Risk." A keynote address presented at the 17th ICALEL Conference, Department of English and Literary Studies, University of Calabar, Nigeria, May 3- 7, 2005.

Osundare, Niyi. Interview with Cynthia Hogue and Nancy Easterlin *The People's Poet Emerging Perspectives on Niyi Osundare*. Ed. Abdul-Rasheed Na'Allah. New Jersey and Asmara: Africa World Press Inc., 2003.

Osundare, Niyi. "Foreword." *Great Africans on the Record: A Dictionary of African Quotations*. Ed. V. Omuabor. Lagos: Omuabor, 1992.

Sartre, Jean-Paul "Preface." *The Wretched of the Earth*. Frantz Fanon, London: Penguin, 1967.

Tumanov, Boris. "Dictators' Kitchen." September 2005. <http://www.newtimes.ru/eng/detail.asp?art_id=899> retrieved 12-10-05.

Ushie, Joseph A. "Many Voices, Many Visions: A Stylistic Study of 'New' Nigerian Poetry." Doctoral thesis submitted to the Faculty of Arts, University of Ibadan, Ibadan, Nigeria. 2001.

wa Thiong'o, Ngugi. *Moving the Centre The Struggle for Cultural Freedoms*. Oxford: James Currey, 1993.

Wiwa, Ken-Saro. *A Month and a Day A Detention Diary*. Ibadan: Spectrum Books, 1999.

## Chapter 2
## Defining the Other

### Works Cited

Abdi, Abdi Sheik, *Divine Madness*. London: Zed Books Lt, 1993.

Abdullahi, Mohamed Diryie. *Parlons Somali*. Paris: l'Harmattan, 1996

Ahmed, Ali Jimale. Daybreak is Near. Lawrenceville NJ, The Red Sea Press Inc., 1996.

– – –. *The Invention of Somalia*. Lawrenceville NJ: The Red Sea Press, Inc. 1995.

Andrzejewiski, B.W. Sheila Andrzejeweski. *An Anthology of Somali Poetry*. Bloomington: Indiana University, 1993.

Buber Martin. *I and thou*. Trans. W. Kaufman. New York: Touchstone,1996.

Casanelli, Lee V. *The Shaping of Somali Society, Reconstructing the History of a Pastoral People 1600-1900*.Philadelphia: University of Pennsylvania, 1982.

Derrida, Jacques. *L'écriture et la différence*. Paris: Seuil, Coll. Points-Essais, 1967.

Farah, Nuruddin. *Close Sesame*. Saint Paul, Minnesota: Graywolf Press, 1983.

– – –. *Links*.New York: Riverhead Books, 2004.

– – –. *Maps*. First American Edition: Pantheon Modern Writers,1986.

– – –. *Secrets*. New York: Arcade Publishing, 1998.

Gossiaux, Jean François. *L'identité, l'individu, le groupe, la société*. Paris: Sciences Humaines, 1998.

Huntington, Samuel. P. *The Clash of Civilizations and the Remaking of World Order*. New York: Touchstone, 1997.

Johnson, John William. "heelloy" *Modern Poetry and Songs of the Somali*. London: Haan, 1996.

Kane, Cheik Amadou. *L'aventure ambigüe*. Paris: Julliard, 1961.

Laye, Camara. *l'enfant noir*. Paris : Plon, 2005.

Lecuyer-Samantar, Nicole. Mohamed Abdulle Hassan, *poète et guerrier de la corne de l'Afrique*. Paris: Afrique Biblio Club, 1979.

Lewis, I.M. *A Pastoral Democracy: A Study of Pastoralism and Politics among the Northern Somali of the Horn of Africa*. London: International African Institute, 1965.

– – –. *The Modern History of Somaliland*. London: International African Institute, 1961.

Mbiti J. S. *African Religions and Philosophy*. East African Series, Heinneman,1993.

Mohamed, Mohamed Abdi. *Histoire des croyances en Somalie*. Annales Littéraires de L'Université de Besançon, 1992.

Morin, Didier. *LittŽrature et politique en Somalie*, Travaux et documents n.56, 1997.

Omar, Mohamed Osman, *The Road to Zero, Somalia's Self-Destruction*. London: Haan Associates 1992.

Rabeh, Omar Osman. *L'ƒtat et le Pansomalisme*. Le Derwish, 1988.

Samatar, Said. *S. Oral Poetry and Somali Nationalism*. Cambridge: Cambridge University Press, 1982.

Syad, J. F. *Naufragés du destin*. Paris: Présence Africaine,1978.

Waberi, Abdourahman A. *La Fortune des pauvres: précis de littérature somali*. Notre Librairie n. 126, 1996.

## Chapter 3
The Chattering, and the Hope

### Notes

1.Ngugi Wa'thiongo's *Writers in Politics* was one of the earliest texts that established the relationships between writers and politics.

2.Ogunde was one of the foremost first generation playwrights and dramatists in Nigeria with biting title like is Otito Koro (The Truth is bitter), Yoruba Ronu (Yoruba Think) just to mention few of them.

3.The names like Alafin Aiodun , Gaha Bashorun are monarch representative in the precolonial Nigeria while the like of Gowon, Babangide and Abacha are representative of the military junta in the postcolonial Nigeria.

4 ."Iwori otura" is from the literary corpus of Ifa poetry.

5.Femi Fatoba in his thesis quotes one Chief Bagunbe, on Ifa in the verse of Iwori otura, Keke, as saying that: The name of the male character, is the Yoruba "spindle" while Olomijo stands for "cotton". The  spindle is a phallic object while the cotton, soft and cushioning, represents the female.

## Works Cited

Achebe, Chinua. "The African Writer and The Biafran Cause" *Morning Yet on Creation Day*. London. Heinemann, 1975.

Boal, Augusto. *Theatre of the Oppressed*. (trans.) Charles, A. et al. New   York: Urriens Books, 1979.

Brecht, Bertolt. *Brecht on Theatre- Theatre: The Development of an Aesthetic*. Ed. & Trans. John Willett. London: Methuen; New York Hill andd Wang, 1974.

Chantman, Seymour (ed.) *Literary Style: A Symposium*. London & New   York: Oxford Univ. Press, 1971.

Dunton, Chris. *New Perspective on African Literature, 5*. London Hans Zells Publishers, 1992.

Etherthon, Micheal. *The Development of African Drama*. London: Hutchison University. Literary for Africa, 1982.

Gbilekaa, Saint. "Radical Theatre in Nigeria (1970-1987)". Ph.D. Thesis, Department of Theatre Arts, University of Ibadan, 1998

Izevbaye, Dan (1971) "Criticism & Literature in Africa" Ed. Christopher Heywood. *Perspective on African Literature*. London Univ. Press, 1998.

Lesser, S. O. *Fiction and Unconsciousness*. Boston. Beacon Press, 1957. Obafemi, Olu " Revolutionary Aesthetics In Recent Nigerian Theatre." *African Literature Today, No. 12*, (1982).

Osofisan, Femi. *The Chattering and the Song*, Ibadan: Bio Educational Service Limited, 1977.

Ola, Rotimi. *Hopes of the Living Dead*, Ibadan: Heinemann Educational Books. 1984.

Smith, Jessie. "Images of Blacks in American Culture" *A Reference Guide to Information Sources*. New York, Greenwood Press, 1988.

Tse Tung Mao. *Talks at the Yenan Forum On Literature*. Mao Tse Tung Literature and Art, Peking, Foreign Language Press, 1967.

Udenwa, Chuzzy "Interview with Ola Rotimi". *The Sunday Guardian*, June 23 1985.

Wasiolek Edward. "Texts are Made and Not Given: A Response to a Critique." *Critical Inquiry, Vol. 2, No 2, 386-391*, (Winter 1975)

Wa Thiong'o Ngugi. *Writer in Politics*. London: Heinemann, 1981.

Wilkinson, Doris. "Racial Socialisation through Children: A Sociohistorical Examination" *Journal of Black Studies 5*: 1974 (96-109).

## Chapter 4
## A Handcuff to History

### Works Cited

Adediran, Abiodun. *The Problem with the Past*. Ile-Ife: Obafemi Awolowo University Press, 2002.

Adekoya, Segun. "The A/Morality of International Relations in Soyinka's A Play of Giants." Moji Olateju and Lekan Oyeleye (Eds), *Perspectives on Language and Literature*.Ile-Ife: Obafemi Awolowo University Press, 2005, 285-301.

Agbor, Sarah. "Memory and Trauma in John Nkemngong Nkengasong's Across the Mongolo. *Journal of African Literature and Culture.4*, 2007, 187-204.

Aijaz, Ahmad. In Theory: Classes, Nations Literatures. London: Verso, 1992.

Alao, Abiodun. "The Message from the Mess: The Past in the Present and Future of West African Security". *Ife Journal of History*, 4.2, 2007,189-203.

Bello, Idaevbor. "A Gathering Fear as Olu Oguibe's Thesis for Change." *The African Journal of New Poetry*, 4 ,2007, 101-121.

Chabad, Patrick. "The African Crisis: Context and Interpretation." *Postcolonial Identities in Africa*. Eds. Richard Webner and Terence Ranger, London: Longman, 1996, 29-54.

Chinweizu. *The West and the Rest of Us*. New York: Random House, 1978.

Clarke, Becky. "The African Writers Series- Celebrating Forty Years of Publishing Distinction." *Research in African Literatures*, 34.2, 2003, 163-174.

Eagleton, Terry. *Criticism and Ideology*. London: Heinemann, 1976.

Ebeogu, Afam. "The Spirit of Agony: War Poetry from Biafra." *Research in African Literatures, 23.4*, 1992, 35-49.

Ehimika, Ifidon. "Social Rationality and Class Analysis of National Conflict in Nigeria: A Historiographical Critique." *Africa Development*, xxiv, 1&2,1999, 145-163.

Eko, Ebele. "An Approach to the Novels of Meja Mwangi." *Studies in the African Novel*. Eds. S.O Asein and A.O Ashaolu Ibadan: Ibadan University Press, 1986), 182-197.

Emenyonu, Ernest. "Telling Our Story," Keynote Address at the 15th International Conference on African Literature and the English Language (ICALEL), at the University of Calabar, May 7-11, 2002.

Fanon, Frantz. *The Wretched of the Earth*, Trans. Constance Farrington. Harmondsworth, Middlesex: Penguin, 1970.

Ghandi, M.K. *Non-Violent Resistance*. New York: Schocken Books, 1951.

Gray, J. R. "The Partition of East Africa." *Africa in the Nineteenth and Twentieth Centuries*. Ed. J. Anene and G. Brown, Ibadan: Ibadan University Press, 1966.

Kariuki, J.M. *Mau Mau Detainee*. Harmondsworth, Middlesex: Penguin, 1964.

Kehinde, Ayo. "Post-Colonial Literatures as Counter-Discourse: J.M. Coetzee's Foe and the Reworking of the Canon". *Journal of African Literature and Culture*. 4, 2007 (32-57).

Knight, Elizabeth. "Mirror and Reality: The Novels of Mwangi", *African Literature Today, No 13*, 1983 (146-157).

Kurtz, Roger. "Tracking the Tramp of the Damned: The Novels of Meja Mwangi", *Urban Obsessions, Urban Fears: The Postcolonial Kenyan Novel*. Oxford: James Currey, 1998 (111-132).

Maughan-Brown, David. *Land Freedom and Fiction History and Ideology in Kenya*. London: Zed Books, 1985.

Mwangi, Meja. *Kill Me Quick*. London: Heinemann, 1973.

– – –.*Carcase for Hounds*. London: Heinemann, 1974.

– – – .*Going Down River Road*. London: Heinemann, 1976.

– – – .*Striving for the Wind*. London: Heinemann, 1990.

Neil, Lazarus. *Resistance in Postcolonial African Fiction*. New Haven: Yale University Press, 1990.

Ngugi, wa Thiong'o. *Homecoming: Essays on African and Caribbean Literature, Culture and Politics*. London: Heinemann Educational Books, 1972.

Obafemi, Olu. "Literature and Society on the Border of Discourse." An Unpublished Inaugural Lecture, University of Ilorin, 1997.

Okuyade, Ogaga. "The Rhetoric of Despair in Chin Ce's Children of Koloko". *Journal of African Literature and Culture. 4,* 2007 (169-186).

Oyeshile, Olatunji. *Reconciling the Self with the Other: An Existentialist Perspective on the Management of Conflicts in Africa*. Ibadan: Hope Publications, 2005.

Reid, V.S. *The Leopard*, New York: Viking Press, 1958.

Roscoe, Adrian. *Uhuru's Fire African Literature East and South.* Cambridge: Cambridge University Press, 1977.

Said, Edward. *Culture and Imperialism.* New York: Vintage Books, 1973.

Wanjala, Chris. "Imaginative Writing Since Independence: The Kenyan Experience." *Black Civilization and Literature.* Eds. J.O. Okpaku, A.E.Opubor and B.O.Oloruntimehin, Lagos: Third Press International, 1986 (130-147).

Chapter 5
Voices: Crying in the Desert

Works Cited

Almeida, Luísa de. "Nativo versus gentio? O que nos dizem algumas fontes africanas nos anos 1914-1922." *A África e a instalação do sistema colonial, Reunião Internacional de História de África* 3 (2000): 646-647.

Assis Júnior, António de. *O Segredo da Morta, Romance de Costumes Angolenses.* Lisbon: Edições 70, 1979.

Assis Júnior, António de. *Relato dos acontecimentos de Dala Tando e Lucala,* vol. 1. Luanda: Tipografia Mamã Tita, 1917.

Assis Júnior, António de. *Relato dos acontecimentos de Dala Tando e Lucala,* vol. 2. Luanda: Tipografia Mamã Tita, 1918.

Chaves, Rita. *A formação do Romance Angolano.* São Paulo: Coleção Via Atlântica, Editora da Universidade de São Paulo, 1999.

Dias, Jill R. "Uma questão de Identidade: respostas intelectuais às transformações económicas no seio da elite crioula da Angola Portuguesa entre 1870 e 1930." *Revista Internacional de Estudos Africanos* 1 (1984): 75-89.

Franco, Pedro da Paixão. "Álas à honestidade: à sacratissima memória de José de Fontes Pereira." *Almanach - Ensaios Literarios,* vol. 2. Luanda: Typographia do Povo, 1901. 35-38.

Franco, Pedro da Paixão. "O Fanfarrão." *Almanach - Ensaios Literarios*, vol. 2. Luanda: Typographia do Povo, 1901. 17.

Freudenthal, Aida. "A utopia Angolense, 1880-1915." *A África e a Instalação do Sistema Colonial, Reunião Internacional de História de África do Instituto de Investigação Científica Tropical* 3 (2000): 562-572.

Hamilton, Russell G. *Literatura Africana, Literatura necessária* vol. 1, Angola. Lisbon: Edições 70, 1981.

Laranjeira, José Luís Pires. *Literaturas Africanas de Expressão Portuguesa*. Coimbra: Universidade Aberta, 1995.

Miranda, António Joaquim de. *O Eco de África* 01 Feb. 1915: G1.

Mourão, Fernando Augusto Albuquerque. "As duas vertentes do processo no século XIX: Idealismo e Realismo." *Reunião Internacional de História de África do Centro de Estudos de História e Cartografia Antiga, Instituto de Investigação Científica Tropical* 1 (1989): 53-55.

Oliveira, Mário António Fernandes de. *A formação da Literatura Angolana 1851-1950*. Lisbon: Imprensa Nacional Casa da Moeda, 1997.

Oliveira, Mário António Fernandes de. "Para uma perspectiva crioula da literatura angolana: História de uma traição." *Ocidente, Revista Portuguesa de Cultura* 82 (1972): 251-256.

Samuels, Michael Anthony. *Education in Angola 1878-1914, a history of culture, transfer and administration*. New York: Teachers College Press, Columbia University, 1970.

Chapter 6
Violence as Metaphor

Works Cited
Abrams, M. H. *A Glossary of Literary Terms*. New York: Holt, Rinehart and Winston, 1981.

Brown, Kizito. "Gamji College: A Review" Shvoong Abstracts. http://www.shvoong.com/humanities/482602-gamji-college/>. retrieved 20/12/2007.

Ce, Chin. *Gamji College*. Enugu: Handel Books, 2001.

— — —. "Bards and Tyrants: Literature, Leadership and Citizenship Issues of Modern Nigeria." *Africa Literary Journal*.Vol. B5 2005 (4-24).

Eke, Kola. "Full Moon: The Romanticism of Chin Ce's Poetry." *African Journal of New Poetry, No. 4*. IRCALC, 2007 (123-139).

Hamilton, G.A.R. "Beyond Subjectificatory Structures: Chin Ce 'In the Season of another Life'" *The African Journal of New Poetry Vol. 1 V3* IRCALC, 2006 (95-117).

Handel Books. blurb commentary. *The Visitor*. Chin Ce. Lagos: Handel 2004.

Marques, Irene. "The Works of Chin Ce: An Overview". *Critical Supplement CS (A)1 The Works of Chin Ce*. Ed. Irene Marques. IRCALC, 2007 (11-36).

Ogaga, Okuyade "The Rhetoric of Despair in Chin Ce's Children of Koloko". *Journal of African Literature and Culture No. 5*, IRCALC 2007 (169-186).

Usongo, Kenneth. "Pedagogy of Disillusionment: The Case of Ferdinand Oyono's The Old Man and the Medal and Chin Ce's Gamji College." *Critical Supplement CS (A1)The Works of Chin Ce*. Ed. Irene Marques, IRCALC 2007 (111-133).

"People of The City by Cyprian Ekwensi" Africa World Press & The Red Sea Press, Inc. <http://www.africaworldpressbooks.com/servlet/Categories>retrieved 22/02/2008.

Winder, Robert. blurb commentary. *The Famished Road*. Ben Okri. Ibadan: Spectrum, 2002.

"Writers Published – Chin Ce". World Writers Website. <http://www. writers.net /writers/35992> retrieved 22/02/2008.

# Chapter 7
## Representing Conflict

### Notes

1.This is taken from: al-Adīb al-Sūdānī: Ahmad al-Mubārak 'Isā (ed)
A. M. Ahmad ((Khartūm: Dār Izza, 2007) p. 47

2.The Arab-Sudanese "considered the word "Sudani" as a synonym for "Black Slave" and felt insulted when they were so called. Many of them refused, after independence, to apply for passports because they had to register themselves as Sudanese nationals before they could get a passport," For more on this see: Muhammad Khalafalla Abdulla "Mustafa's Migration from the Said: An Odyssey in search of identity" in Middle Eastern Literature vol. 10. 43-61 (1998)

3.For criticism of the British hegemony in Sudan and the origins of contemporary conflicts in Sudan see: A. Muhammad: Nafathāt al-Yarā' fil Adab wa tārīkh wa' Ijtimā' (Khartūm; 1958); For North-South dialectics in modern Sudanese history see: Ahmed: "Multiple Complexity and Prospects for Reconciliation and Unity"; see F. M. Deng: Africans of Two Worlds: The Dinka in the Afro-Arab Sudan (Yale: Yale University Press, 1978); --- "Scramble for Souls: Religious Intervention among the Dinka in Sudan" in Proselytization and Communal Self Determination in Africa (ed) A. Na'im (New York: MaryKnoll 1999)

4.On the dialectics which attend the woman's body and image in the pre-independence period see: A. A. Oladosu: "Authority Versus Sexuality: Dialectics in Woman's Image in Modern Sudanese Narrative Discourse" in Hawwa 2.1 (2004) p. 113-139

5.On the male in Sudanese culture see: R.M. Osman: "The "Gender" of Accounting with Reference to different Concepts of Masculinity and Feminism" in The Ahfad Journal: Women and Change (ed) G. Badri Vol. 15 No. 1 1998 (Umdurmān) 25-47

6.On the figure of the black subject in African fiction see: A. A Oladosu: "al-Sud" in African Fiction: Rethinking Ayi Kwei Armah and Ihsan Abdul Quddus" in Journal of Oriental and African Studies Vol. 40 (2005) p. 211-230.

7.On the sacred mother see: L. C. Birnbaum,: dark mother: African Origins and godmothers (San Jose: Universe, 2002)

8.For a study of Aristotle's theory on conflict see: S. Bickford: "Beyond Friendship: Aristotle on Conflict, Deliberation and Attention" in Journal of Politics Vol. 28 No. 2. (1996) 398-421

9.On this trend in Modern Sudanese narrative discourse. See: 'Ajūba. Mukhtar: al-Qissah al-Qasīrah fī al-Sūdān (Khartūm: Dār al-Tālif wa Tarjamah, 1972); In English: A. A. Oladosu: "Themes and Styles in Arabic Short Stories in Sudan 1930-2000" (Unpublished Ph. D thesis in University of Ibadan, 2001) p. 60

10.Recent studies on the image of and challenges confronting the Sudanese women include: T. U. al-Hajj: Tatawur al-Mar-ah al-Sūdāniyyah wa Khususiyatiah (Khartūm, 2007); M. M. al-Amīn: "Is-ām al-Mar-ah al-Sūdāniyah fī majālat al-Ilmī wal 'Amal" in al-Mar'ah wa al-Ibdā' fī al-Sūdān (Khatrum: Markaz al-Dirāsāt al-Sūdāniyah al-Dawliyah, 2001). In English see: Women and Law in Sudan: Women's seclusion in Private and Public life (Sudan, Women and Law Project, 1999).

11.For a study of intra-gender dynamics in Sudanese culture see: Oladosu: "Themes and Styles" p. 60

12.On the female, the feminine and the feminist in Sudanese culture see: Oladosu, Afis A: "The Female, the Feminist and the Feminine: Re-Reading Tayyeb Şālih's Season of Migration to the North" in Studies in the Humanities Pennsylvania, (Forthcoming)

13.Here I have relied on the translation and important analysis of al-Jurjāni's work by Kamal Abu Deeb. For further reading see: K. Abu-Deeb: al-Jurjāni's Theory of Poetic Imagery (England: Aris and Phillips Ltd; 1979)

14.This is quoted by M. T. Amyuni: "The Arab Artist's Role in the Society: The Three Case Studies: Naguib Mahfouz, Tayeb Salih and